MORE THAN THE

Music

As Told By Patricia Prentzel

By Kris Hinterberg

the Peppertree Press
www.peppertreepublishing.com

For information regarding permission, call 941-922-2662 or contact us at our website: www.peppertreepublishing.com
or write to:
The Peppertree Press, LLC.
Attention: Publisher
715 N. Washington Blvd., Suite B
Sarasota, Florida 34236

ISBN: 978-1-61493-964-1
Library of Congress: 2024913338
Printed: June 2024

Manufactured in the United State of America

Dedication

"In memory of Lloyd and Romaine Wheeler"

Foreword

"Ladies, in what language are you singing?" Finding this quote of my dear friend, Pat Prentzel, as I read the manuscript of Kris' book, brought a good laugh and warm feelings. Fifteen years ago, my husband (Tom) and I became "snow birds" in Port Charlotte, FL. We immediately became associate members at Hope Lutheran Church – a church we had come to love during previous visits. We are choir people, so we immediately joined the Hope choir. At the very first rehearsal we attended, the feisty little choir director chirped, "Ladies, in what language are you singing?" when the diction of the group left a bit to be desired. We looked at each other, wondering what we had gotten ourselves into. This choir director did not have the laid-back attitude that we had come to expect from other choir directors. She expected us to do things correctly! We learned to appreciate her desire for every musical number to be the very best possible and for each choir member to reach the highest level that his/her skills allowed. We also learned to love her as a friend.

Throughout the years that Pat was the choir director at Hope, she and I teamed up for musical numbers. We are at the extremes of musical talent. She is a well-recognized professional pianist, choir director, and private teacher. I am an amateur pianist who plays for my own enjoyment. Instead of treating me as the amateur that I am, she encouraged me to play piano and organ duets with her for church services. We had warm and wonderful rehearsal times, but she never failed to let me know when I was "really messing up the time or rhythm." She helped me to feel like I was contributing to the service.

It was a sad time for me when Pat retired from her organist and choir director positions at Hope. After all, she was only 90! Luckily for me, she wanted to remain friends. Several times each winter Tom and I make visits to her home in North Port. It was during the personal conversations in her home that I began to truly learn Pat's identity. Each shared detail shed light on the history of a remarkable woman's life. The distance between Florida and our permanent residence in Indiana does not dampen the enthusiasm we have for our friendship. The phone conversations always assure me that Pat is the same Pat. She is bright, witty, and maintains the same touch of sarcasm.

My friendship with Pat is mirrored many times over with her students and musical colleagues. She continues to meet with many of her students. Each one delights in and marvels at the stories describing her amazing life. The most loyal and motivated of her friends and past students is Kris Hinterberg. Kris and I sit together in the alto section of the Hope choir, and we participate together in the Hope Players – Hope's drama group. Kris' devotion to Pat is beyond commendable. As Kris listened to Pat's stories, she decided that Pat's life was an unusual and note-worthy one. She convinced Pat to do a series of "interviews" with her. Each interview was worthy of being shared on its own; however, the organizing of the stories into a coherent book was a Herculean task. Kris undertook the task of writing a book that would reveal every facet of Pat's life. The result of that is the book you hold in your hand. Two determined women created that result: Pat, the All Star, and Kris, the talented and devoted student. I am proud to call them both my friends.

You will find love, enlightenment, and inspiration in "More than the Music." Pat's love of family, friends, and music is a recurring theme. This book is not only the story of an individual, but also the illuminating story of the changes in our country in the last century. The central theme is one of inspiration. Through perseverance, flexibility, and devotion to those around her, this tiny spitfire of a woman overcame many obstacles that we all face. May you find strength through her many victories.

Phyllis J. Agness Ed.D.

Table of Contents

Prologue

"May You Always Have a Song"

Jay Althouse and Sally Albrecht

It was a lovely late spring evening in southwest Florida. Humidity hung in the air and the late afternoon sun cast a warm sheen on the lush greenery surrounding the patio entrance to the restaurant.

Farlow's on the Water is a popular restaurant near Englewood, Florida. That night, every table was filled. The aroma of food mingled with the scent of blooming flowers surrounding the patio. The buildup of clouds cast a glow over the diners who were fortunate to have reservations. Even though it was a week night and the time of year when seasonal residents returned to their northern homes, the restaurant was busy—a tribute to great service and cuisine. The outdoor patio was crowded with tables of four that surrounded a larger table set up in the center.

John and Dianne entered first, accompanied by Pat, a single lady. They took seats at the center of the table, followed by Jack and Kris, who chose two seats at the end of the table. Soon they were joined by Barbara and David, who sat across from them. Gloria and Denny grabbed a seat in the center of the table and were soon joined by Dick and Jane.

They were a colorfully dressed, mature group, typical of this region, which is populated by retirees. They espoused a youthful attitude, though their ages ranged from mid-60s to late 80s. With each entrance, the ones already present rose to greet each other with smiles and hugs. It appeared to the surrounding diners that a celebratory gathering was forming.

Seated at the center was Patricia Prentzel, a petite woman. She was perfectly groomed, manicured, and well-dressed. Each person greeted her first and then hailed the others. The wait staff quickly realized that she was the guest of honor and stepped up immediately to provide specialty service. Without hesitation, Pat ordered a vodka martini. John, a jovial robust man to her left, declared that her drink should be put on *his* tab.

After ordering drinks, the group was restless, not quite ready yet to order dinner. The wait staff was informed that one member, Don, had not yet arrived. Cell phone calls went unanswered, with the women becoming more anxious than the men about the missing member of the party. Like an absent-minded uncle, Don had a reputation for not remembering times or directions.

Nearly half an hour passed, when suddenly one of the women exclaimed, "There's Don!" He entered aided by a walker. He appeared to be disheveled, but maintained his dignity and offered no excuses for his lateness. He accepted a chair near the end of the table. At his arrival, a cheer went up and then the guests returned to their separate conversations.

A family atmosphere prevailed, with Pat Prentzel clearly being the matriarch. She remained the center of attention. Gift bags, flowers, and cards collected on the table.

The owner, Keith Farlow, circulated among the guests, making sure everyone was being served well. When he asked what they were celebrating, a chorus of answers ensued, "We are the *Soundsations*—we're celebrating our retirement.

Pat was the director and accompanist of the *Soundsations,* a singing group of two men and four women. Originally, it was a larger group of twenty voices, but the group had dwindled down to a close-knit group of six. Over the years, the *Soundsations* performed a wide variety of music from all eras. The perseverance and dedication of their director held them together, still demanding excellence and nurturing their enthusiasm. Like many groups under Pat's leadership before, she inspired them to give their best to every audience. Sadly, due to age and ill health, two of their members were retiring, so they were spending the remaining cash in their treasury on this one last gathering.

When the food arrived, the group settled into their meals, while reminiscing with stories of past performances, favorite songs, and their least favorite venues. With an air of accomplishment, they remembered the smiles and words of appreciation of their audiences. Not wanting to part, they lingered over dessert. However, as the sun was setting lower, the *Soundsations* and their guests knew it was time to head home. Due to their age, most of them did not like to drive after dark.

As they stood to leave, the group paused. Six of the women and two of the men gathered in a semicircle around Pat, but not to say goodbye. The setting sun cast a spotlight on their faces. Filled with emotion and surrounding her with their love and respect, they couldn't resist one more serenade. Dianne hummed the pitch and the group joined in. Confident of their tones, they began to sing a song that had become their signature closing song. A hush fell over the patio. All eyes were centered on the *Soundsations*.

May your life be filled with song,
And may your friends all sing along,
May your heart be true and strong,
May you always have a song.

They continued the remaining verses acapella in pleasing four-part harmony.

May your life be filled with love,
May the sun always shine above,
Go in peace just like a dove,
May you always have a song.
May music be a part,
Of the joy within your heart,
May you feel it deep within your soul,
May the gentle harmony of a tender melody make your spirit whole.
May your life be filled with love,
May the sun always shine above,
Go in peace just like a dove,
May you always have a song.

They sang it beautifully, and the crowd and staff cheered and clapped. A fitting finale for dear friends joined through music

Their beloved director, Patricia Prentzel, was 91 years old. Her life was rich with music and led to this point, but it was not the end. She continues to teach, inspire, and encourage those under her direction. Students remain dear friends.

This is her story.

CHAPTER 1

Childhood, Family, and Education

"The best and most beautiful things in the world cannot be seen or even touched— they must be felt with the heart."

Helen Keller

When Patricia Wheeler, nicknamed Patty, the oldest child of Lloyd and Romaine Wheeler, grew up in York, Pennsylvania, some of her earliest memories were those of spending the evening, snuggled up with her grandmother, listening to the Harrisburg, Pennsylvania, radio station. The program was a popular evening of talk and music hosted by Patty's parents.

Life in the late '20s and early '30s was tough for most Americans. Hampered by the Great Depression, folks didn't have money for the luxury of an evening out. They did, however, have access to the radio. The Wheelers often entertained with conversation and light opera, such as the lively works of Gilbert and Sullivan.

Patty's maternal grandparents also lived in York, Pennsylvania. Pat describes them as being "of the old school." She remembers her grandfather as gruff, but she knew he liked her, and the feeling was mutual. Originally, he'd owned a grocery store, but as hard times changed the economy, he was guilty of giving away free food to those who came to him for help.

However, his generosity proved to be the end of his business, when he was unable to pay his own bills and had to close the store. He never again wanted to run his own business. Later, he worked as plant foreman at a roofing company. She also remembers that her grandfather never owned a car, so he always walked to work.

In the summer, Patty loved to visit her grandparents' home, often spending the night there. She cherishes the warm summer evenings spent with them. At the end of the workday, her grandfather followed an established routine. He would arrive home from work and take a bath to wash off the grit of the roofing business. Her grandmother had dinner ready promptly at 5 p.m. He would eat alone, and Patty and her grandmother would eat together a little later.

After dinner he would retire to the front porch and listen to the baseball game. Patty loved spending the time with him and thus became an avid baseball fan. Her grandfather was one of her favorite people, despite the fact that he smoked those nasty cigars. Her grandmother didn't like them either, but she had learned to tolerate them. He also liked to enter sweepstakes and would let Patty pick the numbers. He fondly told her that she was his lucky charm.

Growing up in a man's world, Patty was fortunate to have a close relationship with her father, Lloyd Wheeler. A talented mechanical engineer, he grew up in DuBois, Pennsylvania. He was a pioneer in hydraulics and lectured extensively. She describes him as brilliant, personable, driven, and serious. She remarked proudly, "My father was good at everything he did."

In spite of a busy schedule of work and travel, he made an effort to spend quality time with his daughter. She fondly remembers weekends as a small child when she could go to the office with her father. With no other employees present, she was able to observe him at his work, peeking over the edge of his drafting table to watch him create complex drawings. His work fascinated her. When she tired of watching him, she could retreat to a smaller table close by, and was allowed to play with an assortment of drawing pencils, creating her own drawings. From the beginning, her father was her inspiration to achieve excellence.

From an early age, music was ever present in Patricia Wheeler's life. Both parents were talented singers, having met each other when they took voice lessons from the same teacher, Mrs. Trieble. As a teenager, Pat took an interest in improving her voice, and took a few lessons from her as well. She discontinued the lessons when she went off to college. However, she continued voice training as part of her studies as a music major. Mrs. Trieble and her husband retired to Florida, but the families stayed in touch. On a winter visit to Florida, the Wheelers made a point to stop in and visit her at her St. Petersburg home.

In addition to the radio show, sacred music also played a part in Patty's life. To supplement their income when times were hard, her parents worked as paid soloists in area churches. Many Sundays, Patty attended the Methodist Church with her grandmother, while her parents performed separately at different churches. Patty remembers her mother had a job singing in the Jewish Temple, and had to receive special instruction in pronunciation of the Hebrew lyrics. Though at the time, Patty had little interest in singing in public, the seed was planted for the future. She grew up knowing satisfaction and opportunities could be acquired when performing music.

As a child, she was more interested in learning to play the piano. Since her parents both played, they nurtured that interest. When she was nine years old, she began formal piano lessons. Her first musical instruction was as a student of the elderly Mr. Link, who had also taught her father, but he seemed past his prime to her, so she found him boring and a bit smelly. She frequently caught him nodding off at inappropriate times. He often snoozed through her lesson while she dutifully played her assigned pieces, mistakes and all.

Patty actually missed her first recital under Mr. Link. In addition to school and piano practice, she had time to play outside, and enjoyed climbing on playground equipment. Just before that first recital, she fell off the seesaw and managed to badly sprain her wrist, ending her performance career for that season. Since her parents had already been requested to sing at the recital, all three attended anyway. As she was not able to play, Patty sat poised on the sidelines, wearing her finest dress, her arm delicately draped across her lap, and basking in the attention and sympathy from fellow students and parents.

Frustrated with Mr. Link's dull instruction, Patty told her mother that she needed a better teacher. Her mother agreed, so they sought out the town's best piano teacher, Miss Louise Lenhart. Inspired by this new teacher, Patty blossomed as a pianist and studied with Miss Lenhart throughout her teenage years.

Her parents performed regularly, so as young Patty became more proficient at playing the piano, she would accompany her parents when they practiced singing at home. On stage, they had a professional accompanist, but at times, Patty was afforded the opportunity to play a few numbers in public. This was her first chance to perform in front of an audience and to begin to develop her stage presence.

Patty practiced diligently at home on her first piano, a Weaver upright. When her lessons were scheduled on Saturday morning, this offered another opportunity to spend quality time with her father, because Patty's mother never learned to drive. Therefore, her father was always the one who drove her to lessons at Miss Lenhart's home.

When the session was finished, he picked her up and, as a reward, he often treated her to a Saturday movie matinee. Her father's favorite movies were Westerns, so that's what he usually chose. To this day, she still has a fondness for old black and white westerns. She later found out she was related through marriage to silent movie star, Tom Mix, one of the original popular Western heroes of all time. Tom was born in Mix Run, Pennsylvania, and grew up in Dubois, Pennsylvania, the boyhood home of Pat's father. Her uncle Ed was married to Emma, Tom Mix's sister.

Patty remembers visiting Tom Mix's mother, a petite woman, who lived in a relatively small home. Upon entering the house, Patty couldn't miss the huge ten-gallon hat, which belonged to her famous son. It was predominantly displayed hanging on the wall in her parlor.

Patty has always loved animals. Her first dog came to the family one of those afternoons following a piano lesson. While walking back to their car, Patty and her father came upon a young girl with a dog that was mother to several darling puppies. Patty knelt down to pet the puppies and immediately knew that she wanted one, so she begged her father for one. He cautioned her that he was willing, but her mother would not be happy about the new acquisition.

"How are we going to get her to let us keep it?" she asked her father.

"Just open the door and throw the puppy in first," he replied with a twinkle in his eye. Their scheme worked and Patty was allowed to keep her treasure. She named the puppy, Wags, and fell in love with him. Unfortunately for Wags, Patty's mother did not love the dog, and his doggy mischief finally pushed her mother too far.

Behind their house there was a large field that bordered upon a farmer's property. The farmer raised chickens and Wags decided it was fun to run off and wreak havoc with the chickens, scattering them throughout the field, and ultimately killing a few. When the farmer confronted her mother with the dead birds and demanded payment, her mother was furious. In the dark of the night, under duress from her, Pat's father had to make Wags disappear. However, Patty suspected the truth and never thoroughly forgave her mother for the disappearance of her beloved pet.

As a small child, she loved to play with her dolls. As she was the only child until the age of five, she recalls spending many hours alone in her room. She set up chairs, transforming her bedroom into a schoolroom, where she was the teacher and her dolls were the well-behaved pupils. She chuckles when reminiscing about these times. Of her many adult careers, classroom teaching was her least favorite.

"I inherited my drive from my father and my social skills from my mother," Pat quipped. She describes her mother as more of a people person, a trait readily acquired by her younger brother. She pictures her mother as interesting, talented, and personable—she was fun to be around. When Pat was a child, the front door was always open to visitors on weekends, and frequently friends or relatives would stop by.

Patty's mother was never one to hold her daughter back from her ambitions. When Patty was in her early teens, in addition to her piano lessons, Patty wanted to take tennis lessons. Her mother willingly made arrangements for the lessons. When she wanted to learn to ride a horse, her mother organized those lessons, also.

The family enjoyed trips to the beach in Maryland every summer. Although her father was a strong swimmer and an accomplished high diver, Patty's one disappointment was that she never learned to swim. Why—because her mother was terrified of the water!

Born in 1925, the Great Depression had just taken hold of the country when she was only four years old. She was too small to understand the economic situation in the outside world, but it was about that time that her younger brother arrived on the scene. Many years later, she made it known that the arrival of her baby brother had been somewhat of a disappointment. She would have rather have had a dog.

Traditional holidays were spent with her parents and grandparents. Patty also formed strong relationships with aunts, uncles, and cousins. Although she never knew her father's parents, she knew his sister well. Pat reminisced about spending a favorite week during the summer with her grandfather's sister, Emma, and her husband, Uncle Elmer, who lived in Baltimore.

As a child, it was an exciting adventure to take the train by herself to a big city. Her uncle was a curator for a historical cemetery, so they were quite well off. Uncle Elmer did not drive, but had his chauffeur, Ernest, pick her up at the station. Her aunt and uncle lived in a large three-story row house, which was elegantly furnished.

Aunt Emma did not drive either, so she called on the chauffeur for what seemed to be mundane shopping trips. Pat recalled one trip to the fish market, where she remembers encountering a gigantic turtle on display—the largest turtle she had ever seen.

On the shopping trips, they usually stopped for lunch. She loved going up to the lunch counter at the Five & Ten Cent store. She realized even then that her aunt could easily have afforded a nicer restaurant, but she must have had her reasons for treating her niece at the cheaper Five and Ten.

Her grandfather also had a sister, Edna, married to Uncle George, and they lived nearby in York, Pennsylvania. Edna ran a beauty shop from her home and George operated a furniture store. They had one daughter, Louise, who at a young age was afflicted with polio, which crippled her for life. She had very little use of her legs and always walked with crutches. However, her disability didn't stop her from traveling the world and she proclaimed that wherever she went, people were always helpful. Louise spent her career as a librarian in a junior high school. By overcoming these obstacles and living a full life, Pat was inspired by Louise's independence and determination.

Her favorite family member was Aunt Peg, her father's sister. She was married to Uncle Don, a man Pat described as having personality plus! Aunt Peg was a bit more reserved than her husband, but was a great cook and a wonderful seamstress. They lived in East Aurora, New York, a short bus ride from Niagara Falls. Pat loved to spend summer days and later, college weekends with her aunt, who by then had moved to Drexel Hill, Pennsylvania. They often spent the evening talking the night away.

Pat describes herself as a very quiet child—even introverted. She had a few close friends, but spent much of her time alone. She attended elementary school in suburban York, Pennsylvania, and recalls the long walks to school and home again in all types of weather. Her mother didn't drive, and her father left the house for work very early. With no friends nearby, she had always walked alone.

One frigid winter morning, she arrived at school only to find the doors locked! Shivering in the cold, she figured she was very late and all the other children had already gone inside. She frantically rattled the door until finally, a janitor noticed the disturbance and came to the door. He gently informed her that school was closed for the day.

Her mother must have missed the notice and sent her to school anyway. With no other options, she turned around and trudged home. These solitary walks were the foundation of a life of independence and self-reliance. If she had to describe herself in just a few words, she might say, "I have always been an independent woman."

Pat was brought up in the Methodist Church, and if not performing elsewhere, her family attended church regularly on Sundays. At the time, it was not uncommon during the week for the minister to drop in unannounced for a visit. When young Patty had the chicken pox followed immediately by the mumps, she was quarantined at home for some time, along with her whole family.

Her mother and grandmother looked for ways to entertain the restless patient and decided one day that a game of cards would be a way to pass the time. When the minister dropped in unexpectedly, they quickly swept the cards under a cushion to hide them from what they thought would be the disapproving minister. During the entire visit, her mother was a nervous wreck that their sin would be discovered.

In addition to their other skills, both parents were accomplished archers. Pat and her brother accompanied them to the range, and they taught her how to shoot. Her father also was an avid golfer. He played at a nearby golf course, which was owned by Jimmy Stewart's sister. Mr. Wheeler once had the opportunity to play with Jimmy himself. He described him as, "A nice guy, just like the ones he plays in the movies."

Pat's younger brother, Lloyd Jr., did not share the family's love of music. She describes her memories of her brother's childhood as spending his days getting in and out of mischief. He also could be quite a tease.

One evening during dinner, when Patty was a young teenager, her brother was repeatedly annoying her at the dinner table. He was the type who, when he was talking about a particular subject, wouldn't let go until he was forced to do so. That particular evening, Patty finally was fed up, so during the meal, she tossed her spoon at him.

This was totally out of character for young Patty, so her mother was horrified. Having not paid much attention to the original exchange and taking her son's side, she exclaimed to her daughter, "What got into you, to behave so badly?" For years, her mother remembered the incident and often related it, as she was still bewildered at her daughter's unusual behavior.

As he grew older and more mischievous, Lloyd Jr. nearly gave his mother a heart attack. Early one warm summer afternoon, his mother was startled by a knock at the door. Pat remembers her mother grabbing the doorframe and leaning against it for support as the stern visitor introduced himself as an FBI agent, and asked to see her son.

The boy had been observed playing on the railroad tracks that ran past the outskirts of town. According to the agent, trespassing on railroad property was a federal offense. The local FBI must have been *really* lacking in serious crimes to investigate in prewar '30s.

In her distant childhood memories, the days all seemed much the same, until the onset of World War II interrupted their quiet life. Like the rest of a troubled nation, she clearly recalls being glued to the radio, hearing President Franklin Roosevelt's radio speech announcing the United States' declaration of war. It struck an ominous note in her young life. The following spring, many young men in her high school class skipped graduation as they were drafted into the service. She recalled with some sadness walking to the main road in town and watching parades of jeeps full of young soldiers passing through, unaware of their destiny.

Her most vivid memories of the war years were the frequent air raid drills. In the evenings, the blast of the air raid siren would startle the whole family. The kids quickly became accustomed to the routine and would run through the house closing shades to block the light, darkening the neighborhood to approaching aircraft, real or imagined.

Her father served as an air raid warden. In the midst of the commotion, she was proud of her father's official position and loved seeing him in his helmet. She admired his authority as he monitored the neighborhood activity for compliance during the drills. It was an exciting but frightening time for everyone.

As the country emerged from the Great Depression into the prewar years, Pat studied hard and did well in high school. Self-driven to excel academically, she maintained an excellent grade point and was accepted into the National Honor Society. She knew her next step would be to further her education and she looked forward to attending college.

Though her parents never required her to get a job, she wanted to find employment. Before she finished college, Pat's work experiences during school vacations were mostly in retail sales. Her first job was working at a shoe store waiting on customers, helping them select the proper style and fit. She was a popular sales person and was flattered when repeat customers would come in and ask for her.

She later applied for a job at Wanamaker's, a large upscale department store in Philadelphia. It was the holiday season and she was hired immediately. After only a week of training, she was assigned to a variety of departments throughout the store. She loved working in a retail setting. Working in departments as varied as jewelry to luggage, her favorite part was meeting and talking with customers. Her personality blossomed, and each position further prepared her for a future of dealing with the public.

CHAPTER 2

West Chester College

"You educate a man; you educate a man.
You educate a woman; you educate a generation."

Brigham Young

When Pat left home for the first time in the fall of 1943, it wasn't common or expected for young women to seek higher education. Upon graduation from high school, Pat was accepted as a student at West Chester College. It was wartime, and it took some convincing to persuade her father to let her leave home and live on campus. She felt that her father was a bit of a chauvinist, who wasn't afraid to say that men should go to college, but women didn't need to go.

Pat proved him wrong. Living away from home for the first time would be a first step in a lifetime of decisions, most of which she had to make alone. Up to this point in her life, important decisions had been made by her parents. She was very excited to embark on this new adventure.

By the time she graduated from high school, she had developed considerable talent as a pianist, but her father was adamant that she should not go to the conservatory to exclusively study music. His influence on that decision didn't waver.

Lloyd Wheeler was a musician and performer himself, but he was also a successful businessman. He knew he should provide his daughter with a solid education, which would lead to a reliable profession. For him, teaching was the clear choice. Though it wasn't mentioned at the time, the considerably higher cost of a conservatory education may have been a factor in his decision. Her parents insisted that she attend West Chester State Teachers College and prepare herself for a career in teaching. Music education would be her choice of curriculum.

As a freshman, living away from home for the first time, she enjoyed this first taste of independence. The price of tuition at the local teacher's college was manageable, so Pat was able to live on campus. Living away from home, she acquired an education more extensive than just teacher training.

At West Chester College, in addition to taking teaching methods courses, she studied piano under Lloyd Mitchell. She was required to take four years of piano lessons, as well as four years of voice and instrumental lessons. A course of instruction in band direction was part of the music curriculum. She remembers being required to create marching band formations, a skill she never used again.

In wartime, opportunities to leave campus were infrequent. Her first opportunity was a call from the local public schools for substitute teachers. In nearby Philadelphia, the Jewish teachers in the public schools were not required to work on Jewish religious holidays.

Several times during the year, the school district called on the college to provide capable students to fill in for the absent teachers. Students did not have cars on campus, so the student-teachers had to take the bus to catch the subway into the city. Some of the schools were in tough neighborhoods, offering a different type of education.

The college also received requests for students to teach private music lessons to local children in their homes. These lessons also required a long walk to the students' homes. One of Pat's favorite experiences did not involve the child, but her mother. It turned out that the mother was a professional whistler. She possessed the amazing talent of being able to whistle classical music selections.

Appreciating Pat's talent as a pianist, the whistling mom asked Pat to accompany her whistling performances on the piano. Pat accepted the challenge, and together they performed around the local area for a variety of audiences. Additionally, the whistling mom was proficient in playing the musical saw with a bow. To add variety to these unusual concerts, Pat seized the opportunity to play a few solo piano selections at each venue.

Romance was not to be a distraction for Pat on the West Chester campus. Being wartime, most young men of college age volunteered or had been drafted into the service, so few male students were on campus. However, an on campus military postal service was manned by young service men, but the female students, were not allowed to fraternize with the young men who operated it. As a precaution, the dormitory doors were kept locked—just in case.

Despite the school's precautions, Pat's first freshman roommate didn't last long. She lacked Pat's determination for a higher education, so she was dismissed early on. For the next few years, Pat chose friends from high school as roommates and formed lasting friendships with fellow music students.

Her most memorable friend, also named Patty, was a music student, who was known as the glamour girl of the music department. Pretty and popular, her signature look was a flower worn in her hair. Pat figured it worked for her friend and unabashedly imitated the decoration, often wearing a flower above her right ear.

As she approached graduation from college, now well trained as a music teacher, Pat received her student teaching assignment at a country school some distance from the campus. Since like most college students at the time, she did not have a car, this proved to be an obstacle she needed to overcome. Fortunately, a young man who *did* have a car was assigned to the same school, so she was able to hitch a ride.

With graduation approaching, she had several offers of teaching positions, none of which appealed to her, and all of which she turned down. Her first appealing opportunity came as a result of her friendship with Patty, who had successfully snagged a suitable husband *and* landed a prestigious teaching position at the Holton Arms School for girls. At the time, it was located in Washington, DC.

At her friend Patty's recommendation, she was interviewed for a position in the music department at the school. After graduation, Pat landed her first position as a piano teacher to the daughters of the wealthy and powerful. Leaving the sheltered world of West Chester College, she moved to Washington, DC, where she was to acquire a world of experience beyond teaching those students.

Her college experience changed her life. West Chester College Alumni Association recognized those accomplishments nearly seventy-five years later. In February 2022, when the phone rang shortly after 10:00 p.m., Pat hesitated to answer. Thinking it was a telemarketer, she was reluctant to pick it up, but concerned that it might be a family member with a problem, she reached for the phone.

An enthusiastic young voice greeted her by name. Pat still thought it could be a telemarketer, but the woman quickly explained she was calling from West Chester University Alumni Association. She informed Pat that she had been selected to be honored as a Distinguished Alumni for the 2022 celebration. The caller's enthusiasm was contagious, and Pat was thrilled at the recognition. She didn't get much sleep the rest of the night, as she was anxious to share the good news with her friends.

2022 marked the 150th Anniversary of the College. As a part of the celebration of that history, the Alumni Committee recognized that Patricia Wheeler graduated in 1947, seventy-five years ago. A few weeks earlier, Pat had received a letter from the committee that included a nomination form, strongly suggesting that she should be nominated for the Distinguished Alumni Award, to be presented on Alumni weekend.

As a good friend, Pat asked me to assist her in submitting the application, and I was honored to make the nomination on her behalf. Seeing the nature of the questions, we both agreed she was a likely candidate. Her most significant qualification was the number of lives she had touched, and the number of people she had taught and encouraged, coached, mentored and loved.

At the age of 96 years old, Pat realized that it was not feasible to travel from her home in Florida to Pennsylvania for the presentation. The organizers of the event still wanted her to be a part of it. They sent the recognition plaque by mail a few days before the celebration along with a collection of university branded souvenirs. When the awards committee requested a photograph of her with the plaque, it was on short notice, so she wasn't able to go to the beauty shop. Pat always insists on looking her best for a public appearance, so she and I had a bit of fun getting her fixed up for the occasion. We spent some time fussing with her hair and makeup, and presented the committee with a lovely picture of her.

The University celebrated its 150th anniversary in April. As part of the Alumni Weekend celebration, Patricia Wheeler Prentzel accepted her award.

CHAPTER 3

Early Career

———

*"If I were not a physicist, I would probably be
a musician. I often think in music. I live my
daydreams in music. I see my life in terms of music."*

Albert Einstein

———

Teaching at Holton Arms presented a new world of challenges. Shortly after graduation from West Chester College, Pat moved to Washington, DC to begin work. Classroom teaching had never been her passion, so the opportunity to provide private instruction to individual piano students was appealing. This experience would set the stage for a long career of private instruction in piano and voice.

According to the school's website:

> In 1901, an independent school for girls, Holton-Arms School, first opened its doors. The school's founders, Jessie Moon Holton and Carolyn Hough Arms, were rarely present on campus, but held the school to the high academic standards for which Holton-Arms is known today. The school was located during those first years at 2125 S. Street NW, Washington, DC. Small classes were maintained to afford the maximum amount of individual attention to each student. Only the most qualified teachers were invited to join the

faculty, which was dedicated to the education of youth. However, this school focused not just on the education of the mind, but to the soul and spirit of the girls attending.

Holton-Arms made it clear to Pat that it was an honor to be included in the faculty. Her students included children of senators, domestic and foreign ambassadors, Supreme Court justices, and the elite of DC. Pat quickly learned that teaching can be more of a learning experience than she expected.

She relates the story of giving piano instruction to Wewan, the child of an Asian Queen. In addition to learning to read the notes and chords, piano teachers spend plenty of time getting students to use a proper hand position, correctly curving their fingers. To the frustration of her young teacher, Wewan insisted in keeping her hands flat. After repeated attempts to correct this problem, Pat received a call from the Queen herself. "Miss Wheeler," she lectured, "Siamese children do not curve their fingers!" That ended the discussion.

Living on her own for the first time, Pat decided to use some of her spare time to become acquainted with DC. One blustery November day, she planned to enjoy some independent sightseeing. Dressed for the brisk weather, she hailed a cab and asked the driver to take her to see the famous cherry trees. She was disappointed when the cab driver politely informed her that the trees were not in bloom at this time of year. To preserve her dignity, she requested, "Just take me there anyway."

Unlike her students, and alone in the big city, she had no money to spare. Fiercely independent, she was mildly insulted when her father offered to send her money. The Holton-Arms campus consisted of a group of brownstone buildings. She lived in the dormitory and took her meals at the school, so her first room was no better than a closet.

She had to tolerate the cramped quarters until she was asked to be a housemother to the resident students. She accepted the position and was pleased to be able to move to a larger room. From the beginning, however, she made it known that she would only teach at the school for one year.

Pat had been hired as a piano teacher by Katherine Frost, the head of the music department. Though the teaching position only lasted a year, during her tenure, she was afforded the opportunity to also study piano with Ms. Frost. In her own words, Pat complimented her by saying, "She was the finest private teacher I ever had." However, she followed this statement by also relating, "But she was a tyrant." It appears that Ms. Frost often got her point across by screaming at her students. "Pa-tree-sha" she roared, scaring poor Pat half to death. It seems that Ms. Frost was also Pat's self-appointed fashion consultant, so before a performance she would often order her, "Don't wear *that* dress!"

Over the years, they became dear friends, but if the respect was mutual, the fear still remained in the forefront. One warm summer evening while spending the night at Katherine's DC brownstone home, Pat opened the window of the second-floor bedroom where she slept to let in some cool night air. Katherine's beloved cat took that opportunity to dash out through the bedroom window. Panicked, Pat felt that if she lost her cat, it would be her last night on earth.

Knowing she had to retrieve the cat, she climbed out the window onto the steep roof to find it. Seventy years later, she does not even remember how the cat actually got back in, but does recall the relief she felt that she would live to tell the story.

For an energetic small-town girl with loads of talent and an abundance of determination, it was the first in a series of connections that would lead to amazing performance opportunities. Kathrine Frost had been married to a high-ranking naval officer. Pat never met the husband, but through him gained the rare opportunity to perform at the elite Navy Club.

Amidst her fierce criticism, Katherine Frost knew she had found a true talent. Pat was invited to play with the National Symphony Orchestra at Constitution Hall in DC. One performance was *Carnival of the Animals,* a two-piano piece. She partnered with Rita Loving and performed with the orchestra in the symphony hall.

The symphony was directed by Howard Mitchell, the brother of Lloyd Mitchell, one of Pat's piano teachers back at West Chester College. He was also the head of the music department, so a few years later he hired Pat back temporarily to teach at the college two days a week.

She enjoyed the position, but without a PhD she couldn't continue permanently. Her pursuit of post-graduate education was interrupted by the arrival of her oldest son, Steve. However, she finally earned her Master's degree from Temple University.

For all the years I performed in the North Port Chorale under Pat's direction, she always made her entrance to concerts dressed in an elegant sparkly gown. I wondered what she wore in her earlier days, and not surprisingly, Pat remembered every detail. For the performance of *Carnival,* she had to come up with something to wear, which also matched her co-performer. Recently married, Pat cut the train off her wedding gown, so the lacy dress served as a suitable outfit, appropriately matching Rita's white gown.

Supreme Court Justice William Douglas was among the dignitaries who attended her concerts. Pat beamed when she humbly reminded me that she was the star. She noticed Justice Douglas, because he always stood up in the back of the concert hall when attending her concerts.

Another time she and Rita Loving were asked to play an orchestra piece for a world premiere performance of *Concerto for Two Pianos*. It was composed by Vladimir Padwa, an acclaimed member and founder of the First Piano Quartet that four pianists first organized in the United States in 1941. Its founding members were Vladimir Padwa, George Robert, Adam Garner, and Henry Holt. The quartet was originally conceived as a radio group, with a weekly show that soon became heard twice weekly.

The ladies received a standing ovation for an outstanding performance, after which they took their bows and departed the stage. A few minutes later, the conductor retreated backstage and frantically told them that the audience wouldn't stop applauding. Not having prepared an encore, he recommended they return to the stage and replay the final movement. Hearing the replay of this unique composition, the audience was finally satisfied.

Pat's DC performing career came to an end when she realized that she needed to devote more time to her husband and family. She never really gave up performing, but exited the large concert stage for many smaller venues. She played for equally appreciative audiences throughout the next seven decades. An expert accompanist, she enhanced the recitals and performances of hundreds of students. As a director and teacher, she continually encouraged her students and choral groups to strive for the best performance each had to offer.

CHAPTER 4

Voice and Piano Students

*"A teacher affects eternity; he can never tell
where his influence stops."*

Henry Adams

A great teacher is not always a student's favorite person, but she is always among the most unforgettable. Her advice and words of wisdom can come to mind at the most unexpected times and places. While instructing a student, the teacher can elicit a multitude of other emotions often not related to the student's preparation or performance. Pat Prentzel is an expert in bringing out the best in people. She has challenged and inspired students of all ages and backgrounds, some with previous professional musical experience and many starting as young children. She can find the talent within and encourage a student to perform to his or her maximum potential.

When life's twists and turns challenged Pat, she always returned to what she does best, teaching private students. While she was a classroom teacher during the day, she devoted her afternoons and some evenings to her private students. Pat remarked that "All of my students became personalities to me." These personalities often felt free to share their joys, sorrows, trials, and tribulations with their teacher. She always knew when to stop instruction for a few minutes, and listen.

Sometimes she encountered the worst in people as well. On one rare occasion, a highly emotional adult vocal student let loose with a barrage of abuse. She later cried with shame for hurting Pat's feelings. Pat shouldered the abuse, and accepted the apology, knowing the woman had problems totally unrelated to her ability to sing. After the air cleared, they remained fast friends, often spending quality time, and even traveling together.

Another adult student, Ruth, studied with Pat for several years while she was terminally ill. She met Pat when she joined the North Port Chorale, which Pat directed, and they became close friends and confidants. As Ruth's disease progressed and her body weakened, it affected her emotional state as well. She felt close enough to Pat to feel comfortable falling asleep on her couch, exhausted after a lesson.

Following one lesson, she unexpectedly confronted Pat and unloaded a barrage of problems and complaints on her. Everything was going wrong in her life and she needed to get it out. Pat realized that her outburst was due more due to Ruth's medical condition, than anything she had done. Pat allowed her to continue until, when she was finished, she stormed out of the house. A few days later, Pat received a long letter of apology from her, and they remained friends. As a final tribute to their friendship, Ruth called Pat the day before she died to let her know the end was near.

Dealing with adult students often required the sharing of adult problems, such as the loss or serious illness of a spouse or child. From her own life experiences, Pat could treat the individual with great empathy. Her students also shared with her the joy of family celebrations, marriages, births, and other milestones. Her studio, filled with music, was also filled with love, sympathy, empathy, joy, and even intrigue. When telling a particularly sensitive story, a student knew that trust and confidence were assured.

One of her young teenage students had an opportunity to audition with a Philadelphia area symphony. At the age of 17, she won a coveted spot as a vocalist at the symphony's performance. Two members of the New York Metropolitan Opera were in attendance at the concert. Impressed at the quality of this young girl's voice, they inquired as to the name of her teacher, and signed up for several sessions of voice training with Pat.

Pat fondly remembers the story of 8-year-old Michael, who showed up for his weekly piano lesson late in the afternoon on Christmas Day, which happened to fall on the day he normally had his lesson. He lived just across the street, and so was able to walk to her house. He came from a large family, and in the excitement of Christmas afternoon activity, his parents may not even have missed him. Pat who also had a family celebration at the time gently reminded him that it was Christmas. Undeterred, he answered, "Well I'm here now, so let's get on with it."

After moving to Florida, Pat instructed a variety of students of all ages. One memorable family lived on Casey Key, in an exclusive island residence. They were obviously financially well-off, as Pat was subjected to an extensive personal interview in her own home before she was hired and allowed into the family's home. Each time she arrived at the student's house for the lessons, she was greeted at the door by a uniformed butler or maid. She also wasn't surprised that the girls were spoiled and not terribly enthusiastic about the instruction. On her last visit to the home, a male employee led her through part of the house to a room that resembled a vault. It looked like safe deposit boxes lined the wall. She was paid in cash from one of the boxes, and then was ushered out, but by her own choice, never returned.

While living in North Port, Florida, long after she could have retired, Pat continued teaching privately, and was an inspiration to many students of high school age. She not only taught them, but willingly accompanied them in solo competitions and attended their concerts. She became like a second mother to one young man, a promising student. His own mother, who was stricken with cancer, asked Pat to attend his high school graduation in her place. Pat willingly fulfilled the motherly role. She loves keeping in touch with former students and following their future musical successes.

"Mostly, I had wonderful students," Pat reminisced with a smile. "Some almost as good as I was."

Her own story also revolved around an emotional time in my life. I was neither her best student nor the most promising one, but at age 68, I was, by her own assessment, most improved. Pat encouraged me to develop the talent I never realized I had. After three years of weekly sessions, while we were preparing for my first voice recital, my husband was diagnosed with a rare and deadly form of cancer. With the excuse of attending medical appointments and procedures with him, I tried to escape the concentration of preparing for my lessons.

In spite of my distraction, Pat inspired me to improve, and encouraged me to keep up with our weekly sessions. We continued to prepare for the recital, and Pat reminded me that my husband promised he would attend. One day after a difficult appointment with my husband's oncologist, I wanted to cancel my lesson. Knowing she would be disappointed in me, I arrived at Pat's home feeling unprepared. At the end of the hour of singing and counsel, Pat surprised me with the compliment that I had never sung better. The important lesson that I learned from her that day was that emotion is a crucial component of song.

Throughout her career of teaching, directing, and coaching, she also accompanied her students at concerts, recitals, and contests. Not all were her students. One of the most famous singers she accompanied was Mario Mariani. She met him through her connections with The Cecilian Society. Pat describes him as a wonderful tenor. In his retirement in Venice, Florida, he often invited friends to dinner parties in his home. Following the meal, he would entertain his guests with an operatic aria. Needing a competent pianist, Pat was first invited to these occasions as an accompanist. He appreciated her talent and enjoyed her company. She was invited repeatedly, and subsequently participated as a dinner guest as well.

In Pat's lifetime of teaching, students have become close friends, and close friends have become students. One of Pat's most unique students is Jane, a longtime friend, whom she met playing bridge. Jane has no musical training, but had a strong desire to sing. Jane visits Pat regularly, often bringing dinner to share. Recently, she was invited to join a church choir and asked Pat if she would help her learn the hymns and songs that were familiar to other choir members, but unknown to Jane. After a few sessions together, Jane returned one afternoon, exhilarated that on the previous Sunday morning, upon finishing the anthem, the congregation had given the choir a standing ovation. Both teacher and student were thrilled at the accomplishment.

After so many years of guiding hundreds of students, Pat finds herself disappointed at the quality of musical training of modern singers. At age 98, she is not able to attend concerts, but finds what she sees on popular television shows very discouraging. In her opinion, the quality of singing has gone downhill. Singers on these popular shows are trained for competition, which seems to stress volume rather than quality of tone or diction.

In addition, the culture of the competition encourages the audience to respond to the singer with loud cheers and shouts, rather than encouraging applause at appropriate times. This often occurs when a singer has mastered a challenging note or phrase, and the audience's noisy response overpowers the singer's voice. Pat knows that straining the voice in these performances is damaging to the singer's vocal cords.

She feels that music is moving in the wrong direction. It's supposed to be a method of communication, which is not easily accomplished when it is obscured by audience noise. Over the years, she has seen a decline in musical talent in modern composition.

Many songs from modern musicals don't seem to stand out or be memorable. Often, songs which formerly were melodic are now just loud. Television, the most popular media, has challenged good taste. Since this is a product of the current trend in musical performance, many have accepted it, but Pat feels it doesn't have to be this way.

Pat's philosophy of teaching is to encourage students, listeners, and performers to respect the music and its components. The student should enjoy preparing music for the listener's enjoyment. She encourages her students to perform. A student has to have a goal, whether it is performance for an audience or simply one for their own enjoyment.

Pat is hopeful that musicians will tire of this boisterous trend, and musical training and performance will cycle around to musically pleasing compositions and performances. The experienced private teacher remains a critical element in training musicians for future excellence.

CHAPTER 5

David Prentzel, Steve and Tom Prentzel

In and out of weeds and dirt, squealing, laughing, getting hurt

Arms held out for love and hugs, tiny fingers finding bugs.

Rough and tumble, sweet and shy, snuggling for a lullaby

Who could name the countless joys that come from raising little boys?

Lorayne Stevenson

Pat's first husband, David Prentzel, grew up in an entirely different manner than his wife. Dave was the son of a single mother who was widowed when he was only three months old, so he never had a relationship with his father. He needed to succeed in a man's world without the influence of a father, and was fortunate at age 12 to be accepted by Girard College in Philadelphia.

Girard College was founded by a former pirate, Steven Girard. It was a seven-day boarding school for academically capable students, grades 1-12. They were accepted from families headed by a single parent or guardian, who had limited financial resources. All Girard students received a full scholarship to take part in the school's strong academic program and lived safely on its enclosed forty-three-acre campus in Philadelphia. In the '30s when Dave attended, it was a school for boys only. As was the custom at Girard, he lived at the school year-round. With the exception of the Christmas holidays, he did not spend any time away from school for most of his teenage years. When he graduated from Girard, he attended the Wharton School of Business and studied accounting.

Dave also had an older sister, so his mother needed to work to support herself and her daughter. She was fortunate to find employment in an exclusive linen store. She worked there for several years until she met and married a wealthy business man, William Battersby.

Dave's mother's life changed entirely when she married Mr. Battersby and she quickly became accustomed to the finer things in life. They lived in a beautiful home and she had domestic help five days a week. When Dave finished school, he went to work for his stepfather's company. Dave was working there as an accountant when Pat's father also was hired by the company and moved his family to Philadelphia.

Dave was ten years older than Pat and well established in his career when they met. Their acquaintance, at first, was casual and Dave took an interest in Pat, while she was a student at West Chester College. Pat describes him as being a perfect gentleman, though at the time, Dave was more romantically interested in Pat than she was in him. Involved in her studies, she wasn't interested in a long-term relationship.

She often came home on weekends to visit her parents, and Dave made himself available to drive her back to campus on Sunday nights. On one occasion while driving back to school, he asked her if she would consider marrying him. Not the most romantic of proposals, she was caught by surprise. She didn't discourage his intentions, but wasn't ready to think about marriage. Following graduation from college, she was surrounded by the usual whirlwind of friends getting engaged and married, and decided to take him up on his proposal. He offered her a secure life and an opportunity to pursue her career as a performing artist.

They were married following her year as a teacher at the Holton-Arms Academy and made their home in Philadelphia. For a wedding present, Dave bought Pat a seven-foot Steinway grand piano. Based on the length of the strings, Steinway called it their piano with perfect balance. It was a great gift for an aspiring young performer.

Their Bermuda honeymoon was interrupted by Dave's severe diabetic attack, which came as an unwelcome surprise to his young wife. Throughout the years, their marriage was haunted by these attacks and frequent trips to the hospital emergency room. Despite this, Pat weathered the situation and tried to make the best of it.

As a newly married couple, they had a comfortable life, but in the beginning, finding a home in post-war Philadelphia wasn't an easy task. Their first one was a roach-infested apartment in Germantown, Pennsylvania, but Dave immediately realized he had to remedy the situation. They moved to an elegant high-rise apartment on the fifth floor of Alden Park Manor on the outskirts of Philadelphia. The complex consisted of several buildings and included an indoor swimming pool, a parking garage, and an excellent restaurant connected by underground tunnels that were used in bad weather.

The expansive view from her fifth-floor bay window overlooked Fairmount Park. Pat was pleased to find that her piano fit perfectly in the alcove surrounded by that window. It was a wonderful place to practice and most days she spent five hours practicing. She hoped it wasn't a disturbance to her neighbors, but she did feel a bit of empathy for the woman who lived below her.

Pat's success as a concert pianist, required these hours of practice, so her neighbor was treated daily to a free concert. However, the downside of that practice was Pat devoted at least an hour a day to piano exercises that were required to perfect her technique. Though musically correct, they would have been somewhat tedious and repetitive to the untrained ear. Luckily, no one ever complained directly to her. Pat loved living in the apartment complex, and made many friends.

Although most of the residents were older, Pat became fast friends with Gwynedd, a young woman nearer to her own age, who lived with her parents in a large apartment in the same building. Their residence was actually a combination of two apartments, and Gwynedd's mother frequently entertained with lavish parties. Being a friend of the family, Pat was a guest of honor at some of these functions, and was often invited to play for the guests.

When they first moved in, Pat and Dave furnished the apartment with pieces Dave had acquired from his mother. Though it was quality furniture, the pieces were a bit stuffy, and Pat wanted to add her own touch to her home. Dave was in favor of the concept of refurnishing the place, so Pat consulted a decorator and enjoyed shopping at some of Philadelphia's premier department stores, upgrading the apartment with new carpets, window treatments, and furniture of her own choice. Possibly because of his early boarding school upbringing, Dave didn't learn the nuances of romance, but he respected Pat's talent and was able to make his wife happy in their new home.

As a youngster, living with her parents, Pat had taken a variety of lessons involving sports and physical activities, but because her mother was deathly afraid of the water, she never learned to swim. Seizing the rare opportunity of having an indoor swimming pool on the property, she decided it was time she learned. It was a private pool with no lifeguard or swim instructor on the premises, so Pat decided to teach herself. She admits now that it may not have been the safest activity, since she was alone in the pool. However, her natural determination prevailed and she mastered a self-taught back stroke, which enabled her to swim across the pool successfully without the inconvenience of getting her face wet.

During this time, Pat also continued her studies with Katherine Frost, commuting by train to DC every week. After an exhaustive day of studying and playing the piano, she enjoyed the luxury of a quiet dinner on the train ride home.

Pat was generally a quiet person, spending many hours alone during the day practicing the piano. Her new in-laws were not a musical family like her own, so they never understood her need to practice so much. Dave had a few friends, but she knew she had to be the one to take the initiative to get out and meet new people. As a couple, they became involved in a young people's group at the Methodist church. Pat and Dave enjoyed the company of this group, as it expanded to welcome outsiders. At the time, progressive dinners were very popular, and they enjoyed frequent get-togethers, sometimes visiting several homes in an evening.

It was during this period in her life when she developed a smaller group of close friends consisting of four couples. They socialized regularly, often going out ballroom and square dancing.

Jeanne and her husband, Howard, lived in Jenkintown about a thirty-minute drive from Pat's apartment in Germantown. Shirley and her husband, Bob, the third couple, lived close by. Anne and her husband, Dick, were the fourth couple. Anne was entranced with

Pat and her fame as a concert pianist. She would set up performance opportunities in her home and invite Pat to play and friends to listen. Anne was a talented portrait artist, and Pat treasures a painting that Anne painted of her son, Stevie. She captured his striking good looks crowned by a head of curly red hair.

Though she was not involved in the musical evenings at Anne's home, Jeanne and Pat were very close and shared the experience of having adopted children. Jeanne had given birth to their first child, who was also called, Steve, and then they adopted a second child, a daughter, Beth.

Pat and Jeanne talked on the phone nearly every day. One day while they were having lunch together, Jeanne confided in Pat the distressing news that her own marriage was over. She revealed to Pat that her husband professed to like men than more than women. Howard was very handsome and personable, so Pat never suspected this. Jeanne divorced Howard and to compensate for the broken marriage, reacted by drastically by changing her appearance. Pat remembers a getting a call from Jeanne who was in a panic about her hair coloring disaster. Like a true friend, Pat rushed to her aid.

Jeanne came from a well-to-do family. Her father was a dentist and limited his practice to society people. As a result, Jean had limited work experience, primarily as a dental assistant. After her divorce, Jeanne became involved with Bud, a married man. They still liked to go out dancing, and Pat was also single at the time. They invited her to go with them, but liked to fix her up with a date.

Around the same time their friend, Shirley, was diagnosed with tuberculosis. At that time, people afflicted with TB were sent to a sanatorium and were completely separated from their family. The treatment was characterized by spending plenty of time outdoors in the fresh air, despite the cold weather. Shirley had two children, so for their sake endured the treatment and recovered completely. Her husband, Bob, stayed with her, caring for the children during her illness, but left after she recovered. He eventually ended up living in his car. Pat discovered this one evening when he arrived at her house unannounced, and asked her if he could take a shower.

After several years of marriage, Pat wanted children and finally the couple applied to an adoption agency. However, the agency required that the expectant parents live in a single-family home rather than an apartment. Even though she loved the apartment and the lifestyle, Pat wanted a family and was willing to make the move. She and Dave bought a house and moved to Abington, Pennsylvania, a new development of homes more suited to young families with children. Pat soon became the local piano teacher, instructing dozens of students, and making many friends in the community.

Their oldest son, Steve, came to them at the age of 17 months. When Pat received the call that the agency had a child for them, she was thrilled, but conflicted. At the time, she was working on her Master's degree from Temple University, and she had just signed up and paid for a two-month trip to Europe. The tour was an opportunity to earn six graduate credits. In addition, her mother had planned to accompany Pat on the trip and both women were looking forward to an enjoyable and educational experience. Pat was deeply conflicted when she got the call. Fortunately, the agency was confident in its choice of parents and was willing to postpone the adoption, which allowed Pat and her mother to take the trip. When she returned from Europe, the Prentzels joyfully picked up their son, Steve.

Pat realized she wanted a second child, so in 1958, when Steve was four years old, she and Dave welcomed their younger son, Tom, who was delivered to their family at only five days old. Despite the difference in their ages and personalities, the two boys got along well with each other.

As he grew up, Steve could be a handful, but he was a very good student. He was quite bright, artistic, musically talented, and learned to speak French fluently. He sang and could write music. As an alternative to giving piano lessons to her own son, Pat arranged for him to take lessons from a good friend. In exchange, Pat taught the friend's daughter. Steve also taught himself to play the guitar. Later in life he was a candidate for MENSA. Tragically, his life was cut short when he succumbed to a heart attack following surgery for a brain aneurysm at age 48.

Steve had been married three times. The first marriage was short-lived. His second wife Terry was the mother of his daughter, Misty. Pat always loved her granddaughter and enjoyed the fact that she had her father's beautiful red hair. Throughout the years, even after her parents separated, Misty stayed close to her grandmother, and often spent weekends at Pat's home.

Steve and his third wife, Frieda, remained together for the rest of his life. Frieda was of German descent, and Steve and Frieda referred to their last name as "Von Prentzel."

Pat got the news of Steve's sudden illness when, in addition to her other musical activities, she was directing a stage show in Boca Grande, Florida. It was an unusual show in that all the material was an original composition. Much of the music was handwritten and it took a person of Pat's considerable experience to decipher it and accompany the local theater group. The nightly rehearsals started at 7:00 p.m. and usually lasted until about 9:00 p.m. This was followed by a forty-minute drive back to her home in North Port.

When she arrived home that night there was a frantic message on her answering machine from Frieda, who at the time, was living in suburban Philadelphia. The message related that Steve was in the hospital awaiting surgery something to do with the brain. Frieda was highly distraught when Pat returned her call and had difficulty describing his condition to her. After some discussion, Frieda and Pat deduced that he was afflicted with a brain aneurysm. She told Pat that Steve was scheduled for brain surgery the following morning.

By then, it was too late in the evening to call the hospital and speak to her son. The next day as she waited for news from the hospital, she received a call, this time from Frieda's daughter, Karen, telling her that Steve had died of a heart attack following the surgery. Deeply saddened by Steve's death, Pat had to leave the show and travel back to Pennsylvania for his funeral.

Tom wasn't a difficult child at home, but unlike his older brother, he hated school. He spent his school years in and out of detention. Pat remembers on more than one occasion the school principal had to bring him home. She sometimes feels she should have seen this as a warning sign of problems in the future.

One spring day, young Tom arrived home from school at around 2:00 in the afternoon. When his mother quizzed him as to why he wasn't in school, Tom said that he figured school was over and so he came home. It turned out that his teacher decided to extend the afternoon recess and kept the class outside for some extra outdoor activity. She neglected to remember that the errant Tom was still in detention, so he had not been allowed outside for that recess period.

When Tom returned to his classroom following the recess, he found the room empty. To his surprise and delight, he decided school was over and quickly escaped. A lot of little boys would understand that completely.

Tom was married twice. His first wife, Jan, was the mother of his son, Nick. Jan and Pat remained friends until she died suddenly a few years ago. After Jan and Tom divorced, he married Sue, who had two daughters from her first marriage. Even though Pat was estranged from Tom in later life, Sue maintained close contact with her.

Pat was by her own admission a "pretty good golfer." While living in Abington, she and Dave were members of North Hills Country Club. Before she became tied down to a full-time teaching job, she was able to play often. She participated in local tournament play competing against other clubs, and still proudly displays her trophy from one of those events.

Her parents were also members of the club and on weekends often joined them for dinner at the club. It was a family friendly club, so in summers, during the years her boys were growing up, she could play golf while the boys were occupied in the club swimming pool. They both became avid swimmers and competed in local interclub meets.

Dave never knew his own father, and without that role model, Pat could see that her husband wasn't a very involved father. He mostly left the discipline of the boys to her. He always seemed to bring home work projects and spent most evenings poring over the company's books.

Family life was plagued by Dave's diabetic condition, and his drinking aggravated it. Many times, while the boys were growing up, Pat had to drive Dave to the hospital late in the evening, for treatment of diabetic attacks. When the boys were too young to stay home alone, she had to wake them up, bundle them into the car, and take them along to the emergency room.

At times, life with him could be a bit rocky, but it also had its adventures. Dave's stepfather, "Old Bill," as they referred to him, invited them to travel with him to Ocean City, New Jersey, for a weekend. At the time, Ocean City was a lovely family-oriented town, with a boardwalk on the beach and lots of great shops.

Doud's Auction House was also on that boardwalk, and Dave feared that his stepfather was getting in over his head, spending too much money. Old Bill always had money and a commanding presence, but Dave feared his stepfather was losing his grip on reality and buying merchandise he really couldn't afford, squandering company funds. Both Pat's father and husband relied on the company for their livelihood, so Dave was perturbed at his stepfather's activities, but really had no control.

He decided they should make the trip to Ocean City with his parents, to check on the situation. Dave's immediate fears were realized when he saw Bill making extravagant purchases, spending thousands of dollars on jewelry.

When his mother showed off an armful of expensive bracelets, he was doubly concerned. The Douds were very friendly and invited the group to a dinner party at their home, a spectacular mansion. At the time Pat was still performing and the Douds had a grand piano that she was invited to play.

Following an elegant dinner served by white-coated butlers, Mr. Doud invited his guests to go back to the auction house and pick out a gift for themselves. Pat was reluctant to accept anything, but after much persuasion, she accepted a beautiful diamond watch. There were multiple cases of jewelry and Dave finally accepted some jewel studded gold cuff-links. The whole process bothered Dave intensely and he didn't sleep well for weeks afterwards.

A few years later, Pat recalls accidentally tossing his shirt along with the cufflinks into the trash chute instead of the laundry chute in their apartment. As Dave pretty much despised his stepfather and his antics, she never made any attempt to retrieve them. In the end, his fears were well founded and Mrs. Doud ended up going to prison following Mr. Doud's death. As predicted Mr. Battersby lost most of his money, which put an end to his wife's elegant lifestyle.

Dave was responsible for company finances and had several business partners. One morning when Dave wasn't around, Pat received a distressing call from Don, one of Dave's partners. Outwardly Don appeared financially successful. He owned a horse farm, and his wife raised horses, which she regularly showed in competition.

Unfortunately, on one trip to a horse show, she was involved in an accident, where the horse trailer overturned and both horses were injured badly and had to be put down. This was a life-changing event for Don's family, and may have created a financial crisis. Possibly it was the event that made him examine his business finances more closely.

"We have to talk," he reluctantly informed Pat. "I have to tell you that Dave has been embezzling from the company, and he has stolen thousands of dollars." Dave, with careful bookkeeping, had up to this point managed to cover it well.

Recovering from the shock, Pat realized that much of the time Dave spent working at home, he had been involved in the process of keeping two sets of books. When confronted with his crime, Dave admitted it, and to avoid punishment, agreed to pay back all the money.

Pat had been busy with her own work, lessons, and the boys' activities. She was never really sure where the money went. At the time, she was charging the reasonable fee of five dollars per student for a half-hour piano lesson in her home. She would bill her students' parents rather than collecting the money at the time of the lesson. Dave had diligently helped her set up the billing system. She had no reason to believe he would ever do anything dishonest, and figured that he may have done it to spite his stepfather, whom he never liked.

As the stresses of family life and his career weighed upon him, Dave began to drink more, and his drinking became more of a problem for Pat. Having had a refined upbringing, Dave knew how to handle himself, and never publicly embarrassed them, but home life became more difficult. Eventually, Pat had enough, and when the two boys were nearly finished with high school she filed for divorce, ending the marriage of twenty-five years. It was a difficult decision. The boys were too young to understand the complexities of their parent's marriage, and both were upset with her decision to divorce their father.

In spite of her difficulties and separation, Pat and her sons knew their father needed help. Their family doctor suggested that Dave enter a program of rehabilitation. Pat and the boys conspired to deliver him to the rehabilitation facility. The three of them picked him up, drove him to the facility, and dropped him off to be admitted for an extended period of time. Fortunately, he gave them no resistance. Pat visited him during his stay and encouraged him in his recovery.

In the manner that she has always lived her life, Pat remembers and appreciates the good times, overcame the bad times, and moved forward with her life.

CHAPTER 6

Teaching Middle School

———

*"Once you master the art of facing a room full of
teenagers and come out alive, you can do anything!"*

Chasing Pegasus (A Play in Ten Chords)

———

Classroom teaching had never been Pat's first career choice. Her father
had wisely advised her to seek a teaching career, and Pat followed his
advice. She earned her teaching degree from West Chester College,
and qualified as a secondary music teacher. While living in Abington
and raising her boys, Pat decided that it was time to take advantage of
that degree. She was already busy teaching piano and voice lessons to
quite a few students per week, which monopolized her after school and
evening hours.

To accommodate her private student schedule, she began her middle
school career first as a substitute, filling in a variety of positions. Many
had nothing to do with music. She was recognized as a capable teacher,
so soon was called every day to fill in. She substitute-taught in the area
for a year before realizing she might just as well apply for a full-time
position. She hoped it would be more fulfilling, but she knew it would
offer better pay and benefits.

She applied for and accepted the position of middle school music teacher at the Lower Moreland School District, a prosperous community about a twenty-minute drive from her home. She taught there for eighteen years until she retired from classroom teaching.

Near the beginning of her tenure, just a few weeks into the school term, Pat was driving to school when she was stopped by a police officer. "There's no school here today, Lady," he announced, and further informed her that she was not allowed to drive on the road leading to her school. Surprised, she protested that she was a teacher and worked at the school. It was then that he shocked her with the news that the school had been devastated by a fire during the previous night. She was curious as to the extent of the damage and needed to see for herself. Since she wasn't allowed to drive down the street, she parked her car at the roadblock and walked the rest of the way. When she arrived on the scene, she was greeted by a horrible mess. Looking in from the outside she could see that much of the school had been destroyed not only by fire, but also had extensive smoke and water damage. Her music classroom was included in that destruction.

Since school must go on, the district needed to find temporary quarters. A local church offered temporary accommodations, which was a start. However, her music books, the piano, and all school supplies had been destroyed by the fire. With no equipment or materials, the next few months proved a major challenge to all the teachers.

Lower Moreland was an affluent district and, although it took nearly a year to rebuild the school, the parents still expected a quality education in spite of the conditions. She held her music classes in hallways of other buildings, in the library, or wherever space could be found. These were trying times. Every week, her class was held in a different location and each situation tested the limits of her creativity.

The worst example was when her classes had to be held in a hallway. Students were lined up along the wall, sitting at desks that stretched out so far that when she was standing at one end of the class, she couldn't even see the other end. In the best of times, not all kids are fond of music class, and being normal middle school students, they took advantage of the situation, goofing off and creating unteachable situations.

The situation was further complicated that year by a December snowstorm. The church they were using was located at the top of a hill, when an unexpected snowstorm caused some very slippery road conditions. Snow and ice prevented busses from driving up the hill to retrieve the kids at the usual time. The students and the teachers responsible for their safety were trapped for hours in the building until they were finally rescued. The exhausted staff had to scrounge for snacks in this makeshift school full of tired and hungry children, some of whom weren't picked up until nearly 11:00 in the evening. It was a memorable year in the ordinarily well-to-do community.

One difficult lesson she found in teaching middle school was that she couldn't realistically teach using the skills for which she had been trained in college. As an inexperienced classroom teacher, she wasn't prepared for some of the unexpected situations she encountered. When the school was finally rebuilt, she was pleased to return to a new well-equipped classroom.

She arrived one morning and was shocked to find that the new stereo system in her classroom had been stolen. She also was constantly annoyed by the disrespect of what was generally a well-to-do group of students. One evening after hours, a group of rowdy students broke into the school and pushed a grand piano off of the stage in the auditorium, completely destroying it. College had not prepared her for this type of misbehavior.

Also, she had to deal continually with a disapproving administration. She liked her first principal, but he died suddenly, and she found working with his successor somewhat difficult. The district had planned a large memorial service for the deceased principal, so as music teacher, she was called upon to present a choral number at the service. The middle school curriculum naturally didn't involve any music appropriate for a funeral, so she remembers struggling to find an appropriate selection. She finally chose a song from *Jesus Christ Superstar*, which was a popular musical at the time.

While raising her family in Abington, before she was hired to teach at a middle school, Pat had become well known in the community as a piano teacher. When she first came to Abington, she gave a piano recital at the local elementary school. From then on, her phone never stopped ringing with calls by parents looking for a piano teacher.

One evening, she received a phone call from a local citizen asking her to consider running for school board. Flattered, but having no idea what membership on the school board involved, she agreed to test the waters and attended a few meetings. She quickly discovered that the meetings were very political and not to her liking.

About this time, one of her young sons was stricken with a throat problem and he was ordered not to speak above a whisper. Realizing that her time was better spent taking care of her own children, she asked to be removed from the slate of potential board members. However, by the time she withdrew from the election, the ballots had already been printed, so her name remained on the ballot.

One evening shortly before the election, she received a knock at the door of her home. When she opened it, she found a woman, a perfect stranger, on her doorstep. The woman asked if she was the Patricia Prentzel, who was running for school board. Pat informed her that she was no longer running for office. Still thinking that she must be a person of considerable influence to be on the ballot, the woman asked Pat if she could assist her in getting a parking ticket fixed! Pat unsuccessfully explained that this wouldn't be part of the job, even if she were running. It was becoming an awkward situation, so with some difficulty, Pat finally convinced the woman diplomatically to seek help elsewhere.

As time went on, the district examined its budget and offered to their more experienced teachers, who were higher on the pay scale, an incentive to retire. After eighteen years of teaching music and directing the chorus, Pat decided to take advantage of their offer and retired from her position. She also saw this as an opportunity to devote more time and expertise to her private students, and to pursue other career opportunities.

CHAPTER 7

Travel

"Music is the universal language of mankind."

Henry Wadsworth Longfellow

Pat has always loved to travel. Her husband, Dave, liked to drive, so early in their marriage, the couple took an automobile trip circling the Gaspésie Peninsula near Quebec, Canada. The picturesque rocky coast leads to a lighthouse surrounded by rugged scenery. At that time, they often drove on unpaved roads, and Pat remembers that there was not much else to see. The couple enjoyed the trip, but on the rocky roads, the car suffered damage to tires and suspension.

As a part of her studies towards her Master's Degree in Education, Pat seized the opportunity for a trip to Europe. European travel in the post-war '50s was somewhat different than it is today. The trip, organized by Temple University, consisted of a wonderful journey throughout Europe attending music festivals, concerts, and operas, accompanied by the head of the music department.

Travelers also had the opportunity to visit music schools and were able to observe a variety of lessons. Pat's husband, Dave, wasn't interested in traveling to Europe, so her mother, also a talented singer, accompanied her on this journey. It was Mrs. Wheeler's first trip to Europe, which she thoroughly enjoyed.

The tour began with a night landing in the city of Paris. That first view of the city lights lent a spirit of excitement and romance to the excursion. The tour group traveled by horse and buggy through the Parisian evening, the streets dramatically lit up by spotlights. The trip was richly rewarding but also exhausting at the same time. Late evenings following a busy day of travel or tours were taken up by writing a required synopsis of the day's experience. These daily summaries were to be combined into a thesis at the end of the tour. For their efforts, the graduate students would receive six postgraduate credits.

The trip organizer stuck to a tight schedule, but occasionally Pat did find herself with some free time to explore the streets of Paris on her own. While strolling alone one day, she found herself attracted to the sound of singing. Following the lure of incredible voices, Pat soon realized she had found the practice studio of the Paris Opera House and was able to listen in on a rehearsal of the chorus.

Among the stops was the La Scala Opera House in Milan, Italy, one of the most famous monuments to the art form of opera. The historic theater opened on August 3, 1778 to replace the Royal Ducal Theater, which had been destroyed in a fire. Most of Italy's greatest operatic artists and many of the finest singers from around the world have appeared there. La Scala is one of Italy's most venerated structures. The opera house is a celebrity in its own right.

European Opera houses are generally closed in the summer, but the group was fortunate to be able to tour some opera houses. One evening, as part of an Italian festival, they were treated to an opera in a huge outdoor amphitheater in Milan. One of her most memorable experiences was their attendance at the opera, *Aida,* performed to an audience of over 1,000. Set in Egypt, the remarkable staging included the appearance of live large African animals that emerged from the smoky background. As part of the dramatic effect, all audience members received a candle, which they all lit it at the same time that night.

During one Italian operatic performance, Pat felt empathy for an unfortunate young tenor whose voice cracked while attempting to hit a high note. The whole crowd erupted into a resounding "Boo," showing the young man that there is no tolerance for anything but perfection in Italian opera.

Pat remembers Venice as one of the high points of the trip. She and her mother enjoyed a gondola trip on the canals, followed by a wonderful shopping experience. Pat still has on display in her home, an intricately carved chair she bought in Italy. I often noticed that the delicate wooden chair in her living room was quite small. The reason, she was told, is that the Italian men were small. In those days, one could not ship souvenirs home. Each day, often to the dismay of the bus drivers, the chair had to be carefully loaded on and off the bus.

In each country in postwar Europe, Pat and company found that the treatment of Americans differed. Generally, the German people were cordial to American visitors. While in that country, they visited Wagner's Opera House and were able to attend a performance of *Lohengrin*. Quite different than Italian operas, the first half of the performance was nearly two hours long. The audience was seated in uncomfortable wooden pews. The program included a dinner during the intermission, a welcome break, after which the audience returned for the final acts.

In Germany, as in several other countries, lodging was provided for the travelers in private homes. A bitter reminder of a country rebuilding from the war was that due to shortages, often the water and electricity in their homes went off at 10:00 p.m.

In Austria, they visited the Salzburg home of Wolfgang Amadeus Mozart. Believed by most to be the greatest composer of all time, Mozart was truly an eccentric genius. He wrote in every medium— symphonies, opera, quartets, and other ensembles. The group was disappointed that they could not visit Vienna. It had been closed during the war, so it was not yet open to tourists.

Most travel between countries was by bus. During that period, unlike today, each country had its own currency, and when crossing borders, money had to be exchanged constantly for the local currency. Shopping wasn't a predominant goal of this trip, but Pat couldn't resist. In addition to the chair, she bought a beautiful decanter surrounded by six glasses, each of a different color, which she also has on display in her home.

The entire tour lasted two months, and the travelers were also treated to side trips, which did not necessarily involve study. They visited the Scandinavian countries of Norway, Sweden, and Denmark. In that post-war period, Pat felt the American travelers were treated differently in each Scandinavian country. The people of Denmark were nice to Americans, and it was helpful that a great many of them spoke English. Sweden was on the tour list, but there were no musical events. The Swedes in general were not as hospitable, and she remembers the service in food shops to be less than cordial.

On the journey through the breathtaking scenery in the mountains and fjords, Pat declared Norway to be her favorite country. There they visited the home of composer, Edvard Grieg (1843–1907), a Norwegian composer and pianist. He is best known for his *Piano Concerto in A minor* and *Peer Gynt Suite*. He lived in a gorgeous country estate on a fjord high in the mountains. He composed his music in a lovely cottage on the grounds of his home. Looking back on a trip nearly seventy years in the past, Pat remembered dining in Norway and that they enjoyed the food, including the unfamiliar custom of consuming fish, meat, and cheeses for breakfast.

Pat passed her love of travel on to both of her sons. She and a lady friend traveled to Europe, and she took her teenage son, Steve, and his friend, Jeff, with them. On this trip, their travels took them to England, France, and Italy, but France was their favorite. Steve spoke French fluently, and many thought he was a native. They loved the food in France and Italy, but in England and Ireland, they were not thrilled with the cuisine. The English food was nondescript, while in Ireland, it seemed that everywhere they went, they were served chicken, so they soon tired of it.

A few years later, she again traveled to Europe, but this time she took her younger son, Tom, accompanied by his friend, Jackie, to visit Spain, Portugal, and Morocco. They again observed that the countries were very different from each other. They first traveled by boat across the Mediterranean Sea to Morocco. It was a beautiful country and they had elegant accommodations.

Touring the streets, however, was an eye-opener. They often were met by young people openly selling drugs. The boys were teenagers, so they decided it would be cool to buy swords as souvenirs wherever they went. Although the boys were generally well-behaved, the collection of swords offered some awkward moments on the bus tours.

Years later and a little closer to home, Pat planned a trip to Mexico with her close friend, Kitty. Not as well-prepared as she should be, Kitty discovered she had forgotten her money. Fortunately, Pat was able to help her, until Kitty's husband could send her some cash. It became awkward when Kitty received news that her husband was very ill, so she had to fly home early, leaving Pat with the hotel bill. Pat managed to settle the bill, but felt the Mexicans may have taken advantage of her. She managed to arrive home with scarcely $10.00 left in her pocket.

Pat describes the whole trip as a terrible experience overall. Landing in Acapulco, they took a taxi to the hotel where they thought the travel agent had booked a room. When they arrived, there was no reservation waiting for them and the hotel was full. Since it was already night, luckily a helpful taxi driver managed to find them a room in another hotel. When questioning the agent later, he told Pat they had canceled all accommodations, but forgot to inform her about it.

In the end, she did find some enjoyment in Mexico. It had beautiful museums, so she brought back a few souvenirs. Also, the food was excellent and the ladies had no problems as long as they dined in expensive restaurants. Shortly after arriving home, Pat succumbed to pneumonia and blamed her malady on cool evenings spent outdoors drinking Tequila.

Pat's husband, Dave, was not interested in foreign travel, but he did want his family to see the United States, so he planned a memorable trip throughout the western states. Boarding a plane in Philadelphia, Pat, Dave, and the two boys flew to Chicago. There they boarded a train and began their journey. This unforgettable trip lasted two weeks and often involved sleeping on the train.

Pat had never been west of the Mississippi, so the trip was just as exciting to her as it was to her sons. From Chicago, they left the Midwest and headed southwest, through Arizona, Nevada, and New Mexico.

They made stops to view natural wonders of the American West, interspersed with manmade monuments, including the Hoover Dam.

Of all the natural wonders they visited, the most outstanding was the Grand Canyon where they stayed in the Grand Canyon Lodge.

When they visited both Las Vegas and Reno, the children weren't allowed in the casinos. However, the casino did provide other accommodations for children, so the grownups could have a little adult fun.

Heading west, they traveled towards California, visiting Yosemite and Sequoia national parks. Filled with wonder at the phenomenon of natural sites on the west coast, they took a break from nature and spent a day at Disneyland. Northward from Los Angeles, they traveled the California coast, taking in Big Sur and then visiting the city of San Francisco. Pat treasures the memories of this trip and the opportunity to show her boys the natural wonders of the United States.

CHAPTER 8

Non-Musical Occupations

"The music is not in the notes,
but in the silence between."

Wolfgang Amadeus Mozart

When the school district where Pat had taught for eighteen years offered an incentive to retire to their more experienced teachers, Pat decided it was time for a change. She was happy to be finished with teaching middle school and ready to take on a new challenge.

She still owned her home in Abington, but since she was living alone decided it needed updating and redecorating. With the help of an interior decorator, she enjoyed shopping in Philadelphia at a large wholesale marketplace, normally open only to professionals in the business. Pat's home took on a new look, as she added some unique furniture, much of which she kept with her the rest of her life.

Despite a lack of previous business or any catering experience, Pat took a risk and bought the Cheese Barrel, a gourmet cheese shop located in Willow Grove, Pennsylvania. She admits that it may not have been the wisest decision in her life. However, not being one to shirk from a challenge, she immediately did all she could to learn the business. At first, the former owner stayed around to teach her the business and how to operate and maintain the equipment. However, after working together for some time, Pat discovered that he had an ulterior motive. When she refused to change her religion and marry him, he left her to her own devices.

On her own again, she needed to learn the catering business, a service offered by the shop. It also stocked a variety of gourmet foods. Around the holidays, the shop was a very popular busy place, with customers lined up out the door to buy specialty cheeses, decorative cheese trays, and other gourmet foods.

The Cheese Barrel's business abruptly came to an end when, through no fault of her own, she lost her lease. The building that housed the shop was owned by the bakery located next door. The bakery owner decided he not want the cheese shop for a neighbor anymore, so he severed the lease. Rather than seek out a new location for the business, Pat figured it was a good time to cut her losses and move on to a new endeavor.

Pat wasn't willing to sit idle for long, so she wanted something new to do. By this time, her son, Steve, had married and moved to New York, so she needed to fend off the loneliness. Her next job search brought her to New Hope, Pennsylvania, which was well-known as an artist's colony. The main street of New Hope is lined with eclectic clothing boutiques, antique shops, art galleries, and flea markets.

While shopping there, she noticed a help wanted sign at a small cheese shop run by a single proprietor. Intrigued, she applied for the job. Seeing her application and experience, the owner immediately hired her. She only worked a few days a week. Her previous experience proved invaluable to the owner, but it also kept her busy without the enormous responsibility of owning her own business again. However, the hour-long drive to New Hope began to be a deterrent, so she only stayed at the position for a year.

Her next move was to the country. She decided to sell her home in Abington, but as she was not ready to buy another home, she rented a lovely converted barn. Her new home had large picture windows in both the living room and kitchen that overlooked green fields. Country living agreed with her. The large living room also accommodated her grand piano, which was still an essential piece of furniture in her home. To keep her company, she had two dogs and a cat, who also thrived on country living. Lady, a beautiful intelligent Sheltie, arrived in her life and became her devoted companion for many years.

At the time, she began dating Bill Boyle, who had helped her pick out Lady. He was recently widowed and the father of nine grown children. Bill was a lot of fun, so Pat enjoyed his company. They went out frequently and found they had a lot in common. He was a Frank Sinatra fan and collected his records. Unlike her first husband, Dave, they were closer to the same age. They both enjoyed playing golf and played frequently.

Romance blossomed, and soon Bill persuaded Pat to let him move in with her. Pat is not reluctant to admit that she was still a bit old fashioned and was uncomfortable with that situation, as she preferred that they get married. Bill agreed, and they were married soon after in a ceremony in Pat's backyard.

Following a brief honeymoon in the outer banks of North Carolina, Pat returned to teaching private piano lessons to help make ends meet. Unfortunately, Bill turned out to be a better boyfriend than husband, and their short-lived marriage ended in divorce a year later. On her own again, Pat was determined to survive another of life's big disappointments.

Once again, a change of careers was in order. As a complete change of pace, Pat attended secretarial school and took a typing course, a skill she had never previously acquired. With the dexterity of an expert pianist, she mastered typing quickly and sought an appropriate job.

Her first job out of secretarial school was at a credit card company. The company office was close to her home, so it was very convenient, although a drastic change from her previous roles of a teacher and business owner.

She was one of several secretaries to a young man in his midthirties. Each secretary occupied a desk in a large office. One day early on, she was busy at work, when looking up from her typing, she saw Jan walk by her desk. She had been her son Tom's first wife and she'd always liked her. Coincidentally, Jan was also employed at the same company as a secretary to the president.

Pat excelled in her job and soon advanced to the position of secretary to one of the department heads, where she performed a variety of jobs. In addition to her expected duties, she was called upon to run errands for her boss's wife. Though most of the office staff was quite a bit younger than her, Pat enjoyed socializing with them.

Outside the office, she enjoyed her boss's company, and several times was invited to dinner with him and his wife at their home. Her boss made it clear to the president how valuable she was to him. However, restless for a new opportunity and chance for more responsibility, Pat kept her eyes on the local job market.

Her next job was at Abington Memorial Hospital, a highly rated medical facility. Her first position was as secretary to the director of patient relations, an attractive and ambitious woman. Pat worked hard to ensure her boss' success at the position. Abington Memorial was an independent well-endowed hospital, which relied on on private financial donors.

When the hospital hired a new vice-president (one of six), she eagerly accepted the position to become his secretary. She soon realized that hospital administration had little to do with medical practice and much to do with fundraising. She also realized that this vice president held a highly political position and his job was to make contacts and to entertain and recruit financial donors. She worked closely with him coordinating fundraising projects.

Her boss was also in charge of new construction and expansion of the facilities. She worked hard and proved her value and loyalty. He used his good looks, charm, and influence to excel in his job. As time went on, Pat found out that part of her job was to overlook his indiscretions. At times, she had to ignore some unscheduled closed-door meetings with young female employees.

She was also in charge of handling his mail, and one day she opened a credit card bill she wished she hadn't. It included some hotel charges that seemed inappropriate. She discreetly resealed the envelope and put it on his desk unopened. Following a few awkward situations, Pat was asked to relocate to a position working as secretary to the Head of Housekeeping. She gladly accepted the transfer.

The job in housekeeping management was pleasant enough and Pat got along well with the staff. The staff was largely African American and many of them were thrilled when one day, they anticipated the arrival of entertainer, Bill Cosby, who was visiting a friend who was a patient in the hospital. However, it was a huge disappointment to the staff to find that this beloved celebrity, who was funny, warm, and lovable on television, was rude and unpleasant in person. However, in spite of the day-to-day drama of working in the hospital, Pat found it generally to be a great place to work, and she was valued as an employee.

While she worked there, she bought a townhouse, a beautiful home with three floors. Of all her homes, this was her favorite. The formal entry led down a long hallway with a powder room on the right and a large kitchen on the left. Past the kitchen was a staircase to the second floor, and the dining room was beyond the kitchen. The hallway ended with a step down, opening into the elegant living room. It was a large room that could easily accommodate her grand piano, still a valued possession. On the second floor were two large bedrooms. This was to be her last home in the Philadelphia area before moving to Florida.

It was here that Pat acquired her cat, Cleopatra, the newest member of the family. "She was partly cat, but mostly human," Pat quipped. Cleopatra was her companion for many years. Pat was walking down the stairs one day, when Cleo had situated herself on the stairs—not a place she normally rested. The cat refused to budge, so Pat had to step over her. The large step was an awkward move, which caused Pat to lose her footing. She tripped down the stairs and broke her ankle.

Always one to look at the positive side of a bad situation, Pat found that it was a benefit to be a valued employee of the hospital. During her brief hospital stay, she received VIP treatment, including the hospital seeking out the best orthopedic surgeon in the area to treat her ankle.

As a result of the break, she couldn't use the steps and had to sleep on the first floor. She also couldn't drive, so she was unable to go to work for several weeks. Finally, her boss was so insistent to have her back to work that he sent a hospital van to pick her up until she was able to drive herself again. Though she loved the job, the house, and the neighborhood, Pat began to make plans for retirement and a move to a warmer climate and to what she hoped would be a simpler, more relaxed lifestyle.

CHAPTER 9

The Missing Brother

"He ain't heavy, He's my brother"

The Hollies

Pat freely admits that she was not very close to her brother. Lloyd Jr. was named after his father. He was five years younger than Pat, but they shared a few of her interests. Since he had the same name as his father, Pat always just called him "Brother," and the nickname stuck.

Growing up in the same home, they were very different. Pat was determined and driven, while her brother never focused on a career or profession. Pat loved her college experience. She studied and practiced the piano diligently, and earned her degree in music education.

By his own choice, Lloyd Jr. did not attend college. Pat's father was of the old school and felt it was more important for a man to attend college than a woman. Pat had to prove him wrong on that point. She believes that not attending college was a poor decision on her brother's part, as it was a missed opportunity for him. Their parents certainly would have been supportive. Fortunately, he had a good mechanical aptitude, which always kept him gainfully employed. She also fondly remembers him as a charmer. One couldn't help but like him.

Lloyd Jr.'s first wife, Mary, was a lovely young woman, who already had a young son, Clayton, from a previous marriage. When she and Lloyd were married, her older son lived with them. Together Lloyd and Mary had another son, Brian. Pat and Mary always got along very well.

When Brian and Clayton were still small children, the whole family was shocked when Lloyd Jr. disappeared unexpectedly, leaving his young family fatherless. He was completely out of contact for nearly twelve years. To this day, Pat doesn't know the reason he abandoned his family without a word. She remarked sadly, "It broke my mother's heart, and she never saw him again." Finally, Mary had him declared dead, so she could move on with her life.

Twelve years later, while Pat was still living in Abington, she was surprised by a phone call from her brother. Although she had not spoken to him in years, she recognized his voice. When he led with, "Do you know who this is?" she knew immediately that it was her missing brother.

When she questioned him as to where he was living, he told her that he had moved to Florida. He also had no contact with his son, Brian, who was now grown, had enlisted in the army, and was stationed in Germany.

Though Mary had him declared dead, he was obviously very much alive. At the time he resurfaced, Lloyd was living with another woman, Sandy, who had also brought a daughter to the union. Together they had two more children, Stephanie and Eric. Curious about her brother's new life, Pat planned a trip to Orlando, Florida, to visit him and meet his new family.

In Orlando, Brother Lloyd was gainfully employed installing and servicing cash registers in grocery stores. It proved to be an odd reunion. She first met his new family when they picked her up at the airport. Lloyd enjoyed taking his family bowling, so on the night Pat arrived, he took them all bowling. Not enthusiastic about bowling, Pat had hoped to better spend the time getting reacquainted.

While staying with them, one of the first things Pat discovered and found it somewhat odd, was that the children were not allowed to have any toys. Their son, Eric, the youngest child, enthusiastically latched onto Pat. She figured they probably didn't get many visitors and to the small boy, his new Aunt Patty was a bit of a celebrity. Pat had always described her brother as very talkative like their mother, and often she had a hard time getting a word in edgewise.

Lloyd's son, Eric, was a chip off of the old block, as he was also very chatty. After a few days, Pat began to tire of little Eric's attention and the nonstop chatter. Unwittingly, Eric felt familiar and boldly asked, "Aunt Patty, what will you get me for my birthday"?

Pat replied, "A MUZZLE!" They whole family was highly amused, but silently agreed she was right.

Her niece, Stephanie, was a bit more reserved, but also was fascinated with her newly discovered aunt and made a bit of a fuss over her. Stephanie still lives in Florida, and she and Pat have maintained a friendly relationship over the years.

After her visit, Pat didn't hear from her brother again for some time. Unexpectedly, few years later, he again called and informed her, "We're coming to Pennsylvania. I need to find a job, so I'll be at your house in a few days."

This wasn't welcome news, because at that time, Pat was living alone in her home in Abington. A few days later, the family of five descended upon her, bringing all of their worldly goods, plus a dog and a cat. After the long separation, Pat and her brother were virtual strangers, but the five of them made themselves at home. Loaded down with pots and pans, they completely took over the kitchen and showed no signs of leaving.

Except for her own dog and cat, Pat had been living alone at the time. Feeling the need to keep busy, as well as supplement her income, she had taken on assignments from a temporary employment agency, often working at night. This left her brother's family with the run of her home while she was gone, and she would often arrive home after work to find her kitchen a complete disaster. At best, it was an uncomfortable situation for her.

Pat came to realize that her brother had been taking some type of pain medication and upon arrival at her place, he had run out of his meds. It was obvious he was in pain and somewhat out of control. Tired of this disturbance, Pat took it upon herself to contact a friend who was a physician to obtain his medication for him.

Time went by and Lloyd was looking for a job in nearby Bucks County, Pennsylvania. He had finally rented a house for his family close by in the country. Pat was relieved to have them out of her house, but she still questioned him as to what he was intending to do with his life. His children needed to go to school and he had to find a job that would support his family.

Coincidentally, about this time, Pat unexpectedly inherited a car from a cousin who had recently passed away. To retrieve the car, she had to travel to York, Pennsylvania, with her friend, Bill, to pick it up. Pat finally convinced her brother that he was wearing out his welcome and he needed to move on. In response, Lloyd presented Pat with a sheet of notebook paper on which he had carefully spelled out a long list of requirements for his family's return to Florida.

It was clear to Pat that he needed money and obviously expected her help. She realized his dependence would never end if she financed this fiasco. Thinking she really didn't need a second car, Pat gave her brother the inherited car and sent him packing. It finally occurred to him that he should quit while he was ahead, so he took the car and drove back to Florida. From that time until he passed away, they rarely spoke.

Many years later, Lloyd's daughter, Stephanie, and her half-brother Brian, did an internet search and successfully located their Aunt Patty in her current home in Florida. They attempted to rekindle and maintain some family relationships. Stephanie visited her Aunt Patty a few times and occasionally they would enjoy a long weekend together getting reacquainted.

It had been Pat's annual custom on Christmas Day to invite local friends who had no other local family connections to an open house. Her home was filled with food, friends, and bountiful holiday treats. Stephanie and Brian joined them on one of those occasions. Many years later when Pat visited Stephanie and her husband, Gene, at their Florida home, Stephanie brought out a large box filled with photographs and memorabilia from her parents' life and Pat's childhood. The contents obviously had belonged to Pat's mother, so she was pleased, but mystified. Since his mother never saw Lloyd after his disappearance, it remains a mystery as to how he obtained those family pictures.

CHAPTER 10

Florida

"Florida is a place for innovation,
for prosperity, for pioneering."

Hendrith Vanlon Smith Jr.

A new chapter in Pat Prentzel's journey had begun. It was the mid-1990s. She was still thinking of retirement and seeking warmer weather, so she formed a plan to move to Florida. Her first challenge was to find a house suitable for her needs and at an affordable price. Southwest Florida's Gulf Coast was booming, but real estate advertising could be misleading, especially when home prices were on the rise. Tempted by the lure of affordable housing and a more leisurely lifestyle, Pat took time off from her work at Abington Hospital and traveled to Florida to look for a house.

With the help of a local realtor, she acquired a more realistic picture of the situation in Florida. She started her home search in the southwest Florida town of Port Charlotte, where she found the weather and lifestyle she sought, but the real estate price estimates had been misleading. Not satisfied with value or quality in Port Charlotte, they expanded their search to the rapidly growing nearby city of North Port.

Her home search in North Port led her to a diamond in the rough. They found a five-year-old home that had been built by a local builder who had a reputation for quality. Unfortunately, the previous owners had skimped on a few details and then used the house as a rental property. It had been poorly maintained, following a series of bad tenants.

Pat, however, had the vision to see the house was well-built and structurally sound. She drove a hard bargain, bought the home, and set to work making it her own. The house was devoid of landscaping, but Debbie, her realtor, a young woman of multiple talents, proved to be a great help in making the property outwardly presentable. Pat spruced up the interior with a fresh coat of paint and moved in. Over the next twenty-five years, she upgraded her home with a series of remodeling efforts. Over time, new carpet, ceramic tile, window treatments, and an extensive kitchen remodel transformed the house into a warm and inviting home. As a final touch, she converted a screened-in porch into a pleasant, sunny, all-season room.

Pat loved to entertain and her home was often filled with friends and extended family. Soon after moving to Florida, she had many visits from friends and family, curious to experience her new life.

Pat was not planning to continue her music career when she moved to Florida, so before she left her home in Pennsylvania, she made the decision that she needed to sell her beloved Steinway grand piano. Parting was not easy, but she knew its value and engaged in some tough negotiations before finally letting it go to someone whom she felt was the right owner.

After a brief stay in Florida, Pat realized she could supplement her income giving piano lessons, but did not immediately invest in a new piano. Instead, she spent time traveling throughout the area finding students who were privileged to have her instruction in their home.

On one occasion, a friend gave her a referral for a gentleman who wanted to learn to play the organ. The organ was not her area of expertise, but since he was a beginner, Pat figured she could provide him with a foundation, so met him in his home several times

She didn't realize at first that she was being set up, but she recognized early on that he didn't have much potential as an organist. The gentleman enjoyed her company and pursued a relationship by inviting her out to dinner. He had recently lost his wife, so was apparently looking for more than just music lessons. Not interested in a new relationship at this time, Pat gently put an end to his advances.

After nearly fifty years of playing the Steinway, Pat knew it wouldn't be easy to replace it. Her first piano in her new home in Florida was an upright. It didn't satisfy her for long. Her piano tuner shared her knowledge of a more suitable piano for sale, and recommended that Pat buy it. She trusted his judgement and bought the piano. She was touched when it turned out that a former student, now turned piano mover, delivered the new piano to her home. Currently, the baby grand piano is still the center of attention in her living room.

Settled into her new home, she was determined to find a focus for her talent and energy. She ran across an announcement in the local paper for a gathering of local pianists at the Cultural Center of Port Charlotte. Thinking she may have found some kindred spirits, she attended the program. The afternoon performance of two piano selections was less than memorable, but during the intermission she met Pauline, who was about to change her life in an unintended direction. Pauline was a member of the Cecilian Music Society of Venice.

Eager to recruit a new member with some real talent, Pauline insisted that Pat attend the next regular meeting of the Society. Known today as Venice Musicale, the Society dedicates itself to music education, reflected by recitals of poetry, song, and prayer during their meetings.

Investing in the next generation of musicians, scholarship support has been the main emphasis of Venice Musicale's mission for nearly seven decades. They offer scholarships to students, who are required to audition for the scholarships awarded at the end of their senior year in high school. The Cecilian Society, founded in 1951, at first met in a private home of one of the founding members. By the time Pat first attended a meeting in the late '90s, the society had grown to about 400 members.

Pat initially found attending meetings a tedious chore. However, seeing the potential of making a local musical connection, she chose to continue her participation in the society. So when asked to direct a small chorus of members, she was happy to volunteer. Meeting weekly under Pat's direction, the group showed significant improvement, which caused the society to welcome Pat into its fold. Almost immediately, she was asked and accepted the position of Secretary. At this position, she tried to bring some order to the group, which seemed plagued by disorganization.

During that first year of her membership, the terms of some of the current officers came to an end. With that, the Board of Directors called a meeting to nominate a slate of officers for the next term. Pat had recently become acquainted with a Board member, Emily, who nominated Pat for the office of president.

Looking back at her recent accomplishments as secretary and success as the choral director, Emily declared, "Pat seems to be her own person." Pat was not entirely sure what that meant, but Emily was the type of person who persevered until she got her way. In spite of her brief membership, Pat was resoundingly elected as president. Not one to walk away from a challenge, she took the job.

When Pat presided over the group for the first time, she had to make an opening statement. She began, "When I planned to move to Florida, friends asked why I had come. I told them I intended to relax and play bridge and golf as often as I can. So far, since I joined the Cecilians, I haven't played a card or picked up a golf club even once." Pat was determined to have a successful year, and she allowed the presidency to take up most of her free time.

The downside of serving successfully in a visible community position is that some people for unknown motives are out to sabotage someone else's efforts. Never one to back away from a challenge, Pat worked to mend fences and restore order to the group. She continued to direct the chorus, encouraging excellence, and inspiring a dedication to improvement from all whom she touched.

Another opportunity Pat gained as a result of her association with the Society was a pairing with Maureen, another talented pianist. They teamed up and formed a two-piano duo. Pat and Maureen's performances provided entertainment throughout the area, playing at country clubs, retirement communities, and school auditoriums.

They continued to play together at a variety of venues, updated their repertoire, and enjoyed their joint practices. They became close friends, or so Pat thought. However, she was very disappointed that their partnership abruptly ended, when Maureen, without any notice, just moved out of state.

Pat's reputation as a musician and director spread throughout Sarasota and Charlotte counties. She had never directed a Broadway-type show, but was approached to direct the Charlotte Players performance of *Fantasticks*, which had been the longest running show in Broadway history. She was recruited by the director, Matt, a dedicated young man who came to Pat's home and spent many hours working with her planning the show. The individual cast members and soloists also spent countless hours in her home learning and perfecting their respective parts.

At the time, she was directing a church choir, so on those evenings, she began her evening with the church choir and then traveled to the building where the Charlotte Players rehearsed. It was adjacent to a seedy bar in Port Charlotte, so she was not altogether comfortable leaving the building late at night.

Another obstacle Pat faced was that the keyboard available for rehearsal didn't always work, and they often rehearsed until 10:30 or 11:00 in the evening. As part of her accompanist duties, Pat was also required to round up a pit band for the performances. Fortunately, she had several friends who were willing to step in as drummer and bass player in the pit. Pat was able to overcome these challenges, so the show was a success. She proudly invited friends and family members to attend the Charlotte Players performance.

It would seem that directing a church choir would provide more mundane activity, but even that brought some excitement into Pat's life. Her first position in North Port as choir director was at the United Church of Christ. UCC was a vibrant church with a good-sized congregation for the area, and Pat enjoyed the challenge.

The excitement came one night when the church steeple was struck by lightning and caught fire. Fortunately, a neighbor spotted the blaze and called the fire department. Pat learned of the event when she saw the report on the TV evening news.

Even though the fire was discovered early, the church had heavy water damage, in addition to fire destruction, so most of the roof had to be rebuilt. The interior also sustained quite a lot of damage, so much of the inside had to be replaced. Fortunately, the organ and grand piano were not damaged.

However, until repairs could be made, the church was not usable for worship or rehearsals. Out of all the nearby churches, the Jewish synagogue was the only religious community who was able to offer assistance. They graciously offered the use of their temple and the congregation gratefully accepted. Since the Jewish community met on Saturdays and the UCC group worshipped on Sundays, it worked out well for both congregations.

Pat's reputation as a talented musician continued to spread throughout the area. She still enjoyed playing for an audience and had frequent offers to entertain. On New Year's Eve, 1999, with very short notice, Pat received a request to fill in for another piano player to entertain at a large house party in Venice, Florida, to usher in the millennium. Originally, she had plans to attend another party at a friend's home, also in Venice. When she called to turn down the first invitation, her hostess encouraged her to come and join the party after her piano engagement ended.

Pat's expertise was in playing classical music and accompanying others. Unlike many entertainers who perform this type of work regularly, she did not have a repertoire of popular music at her fingertips. However, being a resourceful woman, she acquired some books of popular tunes and successfully entertained the party guests throughout the evening.

Shortly after midnight, the first party wound down. After playing for several hours, Pat was tired, but not quite ready to end the evening. She left the first party and decided to meet her friends in Venice. Driving alone after midnight, the streets were eerily quiet. She immediately realized that December 31, 1999 in Venice, Florida, proved to be the quietest New Year's Eve on record.

On that night, the calendar was turning from 1999 to 2000, so the whole world was waiting in anticipation for a nationwide blackout or technical disaster that would end civilization as we know it. Therefore, in the early hours of New Year's Day 2000, in a predominantly retired community, the streets were empty.

Fortunately, nothing was amiss. The power stayed on and the street lights worked as usual, so she easily found her way to her friend's home. In the absence of any unusual phenomenon, she quietly partied on with good friends until the wee hours of the New Year. I'd like to note that this talented and intrepid lady was 74 years old.

CHAPTER 11

North Port Chorale, Choraliers, and Soundsations

"Music gives a soul to the universe,
wings to the mind, flight to the imagination,
and charm and gaiety to life and to everything."

Plato

In 1998, the North Port Chorale was seeking a new director, and the position paid the paltry sum of $350.00 a year. Pat considered the position and finally accepted it. She knew it would be a labor of love, rather than of money, so before she took over the job, she elected to attend the Christmas concert, which was the final performance of the chorale under the retiring director. The group rehearsed and performed at a local church, and she wanted see the group in action. When she attended the concert, her only thought was, "Oh, my Lord, what have I gotten myself into?"

She could see that the group had potential, but needed some guidance to achieve a more professional demeanor. Pat's goal was for the Chorale to represent the city of North Port as a respected performing group. She knew she needed to recruit capable singers and recruit members for a larger group.

She dug in her heels and planned for the future. Her first goal was to turn the group into a quality performing group that would attract larger audiences. To accomplish this, her next step was to hire a guest artist to add variety to the concert.

Her first guest artists were a pianist, LaTerry Butler, and his wife. Mr. Butler was a talented pianist whose trademark was wearing white gloves while he played. He also accompanied his wife while she sang. Mrs. Butler had a lovely voice, but loved to improvise, which can be a challenge to any accompanist. The Butlers were surprised when they were asked to attend a dress rehearsal the day before the concert. Mr. Butler was accustomed to just showing up and performing, but he found that on this occasion, he needed to submit to Pat Prentzel's high standards of preparation.

Many of the current singers were retired and had joined the Chorale for the fun of it. Turning "having fun" into quality music was Pat's continuing challenge. Fortunately, the Chorale did include a number of talented and capable singers, who appreciated and shared her quest for quality. The rest of the singers rose to the challenge and as the quality improved, so did the number of singers.

In addition to performing a series of concerts, the mission of the North Port Performing Arts Association was to raise funds to present scholarships to students from North Port High School. Therefore, it was important to attract and entertain a paying audience. As the number of singers and quality of musical performance improved over the years, the dollar amount of the awards increased, and the number of student scholarship recipients grew as well.

As the Chorale grew under Pat's direction, it moved from the Methodist Church to a larger Presbyterian Church for its rehearsals. The group met once a week for a two-hour rehearsal and performed three concerts per season. The season ran concurrent with the arrival of winter residents. Rehearsals began in September and ended with the final concert the following April.

The only instrumental accompaniment for the chorale was a piano, so a crucial element in producing a pleasing concert was a competent accompanist. The accompanist was the only other paid position, but in a relatively small city, it was a challenge to find and keep a good one. During her thirteen-year tenure as director, Pat outlasted several accompanists.

Most accompanists turned out to be wonderful supportive musicians, who used their talents to enhance the group's practices and performances. Her first accompanist, Gary, was talented and supportive, but he had to resign due to family obligations. He was followed by another woman who was a private piano teacher. Shortly after she was hired, she chose to move to Sarasota and resigned.

The next accompanist showed great promise. She was talented, enthusiastic, dynamic, and creative—a real asset to the group. She and Pat became close friends as well as colleagues. They worked well together as director and accompanist, until it was evident that the accompanist aspired to be the director. Little by little, she attempted to exceed Pat's authority until one evening, following the rehearsal, a shouting match in the parking lot ended the relationship. The rehearsal ended on an uncomfortable note when late in the rehearsal, the accompanist tried to introduce some choreography into one of the numbers.

At the end of a long rehearsal, the singers were tired and having difficulty with the accompanist's directions. She took it as a personal insult. Due to the late hour, Pat was not immediately concerned about the lack of cooperation from the singers, but the accompanist was visibly annoyed at Pat's lack of support.

It was after 9:30 p.m. All the other singers had left, but as they walked out to the parking lot, the accompanist flew into a rage and in a loud voice repeatedly berated her. Pat cringed in horror, not able to get a word in edgewise. Every time she attempted to speak up, the accompanist shouted, "Don't you talk while I'm talking!" Alone in the poorly lit parking lot, Pat was intimidated, even frightened, and reluctantly took the abuse.

Finally, the accompanist ended the confrontation, got into her car, and tore out of the parking lot, squealing her tires. Badly shaken, Pat drove home and immediately reached out to the president of the Chorale and demanded the accompanist's resignation. The president agreed and that was the end of the incident. Disappointed to lose a competent accompanist and one she had thought was a close friend, Pat moved on.

Unfortunately, this wasn't her only unpleasant encounter as director of the Chorale. In the performance of her duties as leader of the group, Pat was invited by a local organization to a dinner to recognize her success as director of the Chorale. When Pat first attended meetings of the Cecilian Society, she had been warned about one of the members by more than one person. "Don't get involved with her," they whispered behind the scenes.

Being new in town, Pat disregarded their warnings and felt she could make her own character judgement. At the dinner, in front of everyone, this same person, who had invited Pat to the dinner, proceeded to belittle Pat and would not let her speak or graciously accept the accolades that she deserved. They rode home together in an awkward silence, and Pat never saw her again.

As word got out locally that the Chorale had become a quality group, membership increased. So that they would be placed in the correct voice section, prospective members were subjected to a brief audition, usually at their first appearance at a rehearsal.

In the early days of the season, new members were lined up outside the door, waiting for an audition. To save rehearsal time, sometimes they were invited to sing with the group and audition later. Pat was a diligent recruiter. If she heard a voice she liked in her church congregation or elsewhere, she sent out her scouts to encourage that singer to join her Chorale.

The Chorale continued to consist of a few semiprofessional singers, former and current teachers, and some directors of other choral and instrumental groups. Still, the majority of the participants were a lively group of senior citizens, who just liked to sing. All the members had previous experience in other choral groups, but few had formal training. Pat had the unique gift of seeing potential in musicians who could not see it in themselves.

In the early 2000s, the city of North Port was experiencing considerable growth. As the community expanded, the Chorale continued to grow. Rehearsals and performances moved to the North Port Performing Arts Center, a new facility adjacent to the high school, but built for the use of the community concert band, symphony orchestra, and Chorale. During the planning and construction, Pat met several times with the architect. Her input was valuable in planning a performance hall with acoustics suitable for individuals and groups.

By 2005, the North Port Chorale was a vibrant 80-voice community chorus which acquired most members by word of mouth, many of whom had attended a concert and had a desire to join. At Pat's invitation, I became voice number 81.

As director of the Chorale, her main challenge was to choose musical selections that were within the singer's collective abilities. It was also important that they be entertaining to an audience of local family and friends. She spent endless hours compiling selections for the upcoming show. Each concert had a theme, so the numbers were chosen to fit that theme as well.

The December concert, the first of the season, regularly followed a Christmas theme, combining secular and sacred selections. An annual challenge was finding a selection that celebrated Hanukkah as well. Traditional wintry tunes contrasted with contemporary versions of old favorites. Each year, the concert concluded with a rousing rendition of Handel's Hallelujah Chorus. Pat liked to challenge the singers and keep the concerts fresh, so this was nearly the only time Pat ever repeated a selection.

Holding the attention of a diverse group of singers and challenging their voices to the fullest potential required two hours of focused energy. By now, Pat was well into her 70s and never faltered in that direction. She did not hand out frivolous compliments. During early rehearsals, after a particularly painful rendition of a section of a song, she would firmly state, "That was awful," followed by her signature stony glare, referred by the singers as, "The Look."

When diction was sloppy and the words were indecipherable, she would remark, "What language are you singing in?" The group, chastised, would settle into fierce concentration and by the end of the evening, they would achieve the ultimate compliment of, "That's a little better—now take this music home and learn it!"

By the end of the night, the glare always softened into a smile and encouraging words. In concert, under Pat Prentzel's direction, the North Port Chorale continued to attract larger audiences. Pat inspired them to look and act professional and to give every audience the performance they deserved.

In contrast to the large number of retirees, the Chorale was often peppered with some young singers of high school age. As a result of the scholarship program, high school students were encouraged to join the Chorale, which allowed the scholarship committee to notice them.

Recognizing this young talent, Pat encouraged and offered private training to these students. She enjoyed following their continuing education and careers for years. At one time, she had as many as seven college students majoring in voice who were taking weekly private lessons with her.

To continue to add variety and interest to the performances, Pat created a select group within the larger Chorale, which was named the *Choraliers*. This group consisted of twenty singers who had an ability to read music and were willing to attend additional rehearsal time.

The *Choraliers* performed special numbers at the three scheduled concerts and then sought additional performance opportunities throughout North Port and surrounding communities. They served as ambassadors for the Chorale at community events. Pat was able to challenge this group with more difficult music, continually adding to their repertoire.

Seeking their own identity, the *Choraliers* chose a new name, the *Soundsations*. Pat continued to encourage excellence, and the singers adapted more of a show choir style, memorizing music, and adding choreography. I was privileged to be a member of this group.

After thirteen seasons, Pat retired from the director position of the Chorale, but she chose to remain as director of the *Soundsations*. Even though a member of *the Soundsations* was required to be a member of the Chorale, and under the scrutiny of the Board of Directors, Pat realized she was once again on her own. There was only token support from the Chorale director who replaced her.

As usual, Pat never let that hinder her efforts. As a smaller group under Pat's direction, the *Soundsations* obtained an identity of their own and became a performing group that entertained at different occasions and locations throughout the community. They had repeat requests from several venues, and were able to charge a fee for performances. All proceeds went back to the treasury of the Chorale to invest in equipment and contribute to scholarship funds.

For three years, Pat enjoyed directing the *Soundsations,* and realized that a special camaraderie had formed within the members. Her goal of excellence never faltered. Though all the singers were in their 60s or 70s, with a few in their 80s, she inspired them to retain their youthful enthusiasm. Their costumes and repertoire varied greatly.

One week, they participated at the grand opening of a gas station, singing outside with a keyboard, wearing colorful t-shirts and flips flops. Soon afterward, dressed in tuxes and evening gowns, they appeared before a full house at the Performing Arts Center, accompanied by a grand piano and percussion.

To encourage that never-ending pursuit of musical quality, Pat offered each member a free private voice lesson, hoping he or she would continue the training. She wanted to demonstrate the value of ongoing training and regular practice at any age. That was when I became her vocal student.

Due to budget constraints, when the Board of Directors of the Chorale no longer wished to recognize the *Soundsations* as a group and withdrew their financial support, Pat did not want the group to disband. Dedicated to that cause, she moved rehearsals to her home and continued to direct and accompany them without compensation.

Soundsations were now clearly an independent performing group and remained together for several more years, bringing entertainment to elderly groups and civic organizations throughout the area. When the group finally dwindled to six dedicated singers, Pat encouraged each person to perform solos or duets of their own choice to round out each performance.

When Pat's family planned her 90th birthday celebration, they requested the *Soundsations* make an appearance. Pat and her family were welcomed back to Hope Lutheran Church, where Pat had directed the choir. Following a celebratory meal in the church's fellowship hall, the festivities moved to the sanctuary. As always, there was no respite for the guest of honor. In a room filled with family and friends, Pat proceeded to direct and accompany a razzle-dazzle performance.

The sanctuary was transformed for the afternoon into a cabaret atmosphere, where the singers simulated a reunion of old friends getting together to reminisce. Sipping a glass of what looked like champagne, but tasted like ginger ale, each one told a bit of his or her own life story, which segued into a song. The show allowed each singer to showcase his or her specialty. They entertained family and friends with song, dance, and humor. Pat never ceased to bring out the best in everyone.

Many former members of the Chorale and *Soundsations* attended the party. As a finale, and to honor her birthday, they all joined together in wrapping up the show with a group rendition of their unofficial theme song, *May You Always Have a Song*. Reluctant to end the day, everyone lingered afterwards to reminisce with stories of the hard work, good times, and great friendships brought together in the performance of a favorite song.

CHAPTER 12

Hope Lutheran Church

*"I play the notes as they are written,
but it is God who makes the music."*

Johann Sebastian Bach

Pat has been a woman of faith since her early childhood. We first became acquainted when she took a job as the organist and choir director at Hope Lutheran Church. Hope is a small congregation in Port Charlotte, Florida. When their current organist resigned, the church's music committee placed an ad in the local newspaper for a replacement. Dissatisfied with her current church choir director position, Pat answered the ad.

The committee quickly realized that they could acquire a jewel of a director and she was hired on the spot. The salary was minimal for a person of her talent and experience, so once again, Pat realized she had taken the position for the love of the job.

She also realized that, based on the demographics and size and location of the congregation, it never would have the potential to become a lucrative position. Fortunately for the congregation, she accepted the position and soon played her way into the hearts of the congregation. In her decade of service, she formed lifetime friendships with many of the members.

Lending her talents to occasions joyous and sad, she became a part of the church family. The congregation was made up mostly of retired people who, like Pat, had moved to Florida for the warm weather and relaxed lifestyle. "In the beginning," Pat mused, "there seemed to be a funeral every other week." Pat received a request to play the organ at most of those occasions.

Making changes to a traditional house of worship requires some diplomacy. Pat immediately realized that the placement of the organ, piano, and seating area of the choir were not to her liking. There was no budget to hire an accompanist, so the job of choir director also included accompanying the choir on the piano. Since she was not satisfied with the current seating, she carefully rearranged the position of organ and choir seating area. One might have thought the change was for musical effectiveness, but Pat had an additional motive.

Along with their new casual lifestyle, some participants did not feel the need to dress up for church. Pat felt that a choir should maintain some semblance of decorum. The choir sat front and center facing the congregation, and Pat determined that shorts and flip flops were inappropriate choir apparel. Her new seating arrangement helped the choir to be a bit less obvious and more presentable. She remedied the situation further, when the pastor received a monetary bequest and asked Pat if she had any requests. Without hesitation she exclaimed, "New choir robes!" It was important to her that her singers looked like a choir, as well as sounding like one.

The Lutheran liturgy is filled with pastoral readings and musical responses by the congregation. At the time, the church was experiencing a transitional period between using older, more conservative music and some more contemporary. Pat quipped that her arms would get tired, not only of playing continually throughout the service, but she needed to quickly switch from one heavy service book to another.

During the prelude and postlude to the service, Pat could choose from her vast repertoire of sacred music and the congregation could be treated to a mini organ concert at the beginning or end of each service. From time to time at the end of the service, the congregation erupted in applause, a behavior not usually condoned by a more traditional Lutheran congregation.

Each organ has its own characteristics, but when Pat first appeared on the scene, the organ manual had mysteriously disappeared. In the first few weeks of her service, Pat was able to produce properly appropriate church music, but had not had an opportunity investigate all the intricacies of the instrument.

She admits now that she really did not know how to play the organ, but she practiced for several hours each week and soon had mastered the church organ. In her own words, "You just can't play an organ— you must become acquainted with it." However, the members of the church were quite satisfied with her work.

Periodically, an organ technician was on call to perform scheduled maintenance. Without her knowledge, he was scheduled to work the week preceding the funeral service of a beloved church member. The technician liked to adjust the organ settings, and being very familiar with the instrument, he needed no manual to put the organ through a variety of instrumental sounds. Finishing his tuneup, he proceeded to entertain himself and anyone within earshot with a boisterous concert.

The funeral was on a dismal rainy morning and the small church was packed with family and friends of the deceased. A large group of church members also attended. The solemn occasion offered no opportunity for warmup or prelude, so Pat quietly powered up the organ and waited for her cue.

The pastor began the service with a warm welcome and prayer. Next, the program listed a hymn. Pat customarily played an introductory verse before the singers joined in. To her shock and everyone else's, the organ's voice had been transformed to sound like a harpsichord, with the volume turned up to a deafening level.

The consummate professional, Pat paused a moment to collect her thoughts, restore the volume to normal, and continued to play the hymn on the harpsichord-sounding organ, as though that was the plan. The mourners joined in song and sang several verses of that old favorite hymn.

Following the hymn, one could hear murmuring throughout the congregation that it was quite a creative touch from the new organist, or possibly had been an unusual request of the deceased. Though it was not funny at the time, we still have a good laugh about it every time we think of it. During the eulogies, Pat managed to restore the organ to its original settings and the service concluded without further incident.

Pat and I entered the Hope choir at the same time, with her as the director and accompanist, and me as an enthusiastic, but unrefined singer. Choir practice was a never-ending challenge. At its peak, the group had as many as twenty members, most of them also enthusiastic and unrefined.

By request of the music committee and the pastor, the choir was asked to offer an anthem each week. The choir was accustomed to meeting on Sunday morning to review the anthem for the morning and then break in a new one for the following week. A weekday evening rehearsal was pretty much out of the question. Many of these folks did not care to drive at night, but it was obvious to Pat that most of the members did not practice at home on their own.

Despite continual reminders, Pat rarely knew ahead of time what singers would appear for the Sunday 8:30 a.m. practice to prepare for the 10:00 service. It was an ongoing challenge to be fully prepared. Working within these limitations, she chose appropriate anthems for the season, and demanded the best from everyone.

When it was time for the choir to sing during the service, she had to climb down from the organ, slide in behind the piano, and direct with her head and eyes. The choir quickly learned that she has the most expressive eyes! We all just loved to sing, and the congregation generally appreciated our musical offerings. Making the best of our efforts, she shaped that enthusiasm into an acceptable musical offering.

The choir season began that year on the first of October with the arrival of our snow birds and lasted until the end of April with their departure. There were special performances during Advent, Christmas, Holy Week, and Easter. Towards the end of this long season, one of the more boisterous basses stopped Pat after church one Sunday and contritely asked if she might point out which line of music he was supposed to be singing. She patiently pointed out the correct part and kindly kept her comments to herself.

During her ten years of service, she outlasted one long-serving pastor, but when he resigned, she had to work with a series of temporary replacements. Each new interim pastor had his own agenda of preparing the congregation for a change. To that end, each one challenged Pat with his own special touches to the service. She spent her final year of service to the congregation attempting to meet those demands, and often adapting at the last minute to the unexpected modifications.

Friends formed during those years still check on her health regularly. One special friendship was with Arline, the wife of a retired pastor, who had been a member of the selection committee when Pat was hired. She had been a dedicated choir member and an active church member.

Arline and Pat were close in age and became dear friends. They enjoyed frequent social evenings, which usually included Arline's husband, Pastor Ed. During one especially memorable evening as they were awaiting service at a restaurant, in an animated discussion, Arline accidently bumped her glass of ice water. It splashed across the table and soaked Pat.

The restaurant air conditioning exacerbated the situation, but despite the fact that Pat was soaked and shivering and Arline was mortified, the meal continued. As good friends will, they laughed about it many times. Arline's demeanor as a pastor's wife led others in the congregaton to believe that she was very strait-laced. Her husband however had displayed his wry sense of humor, and many times during his sermons, he caught the congregation off guard.

One time when Pastor Ed was filling in for the vacationing pastor, he mentioned that he was sorry his wife couldn't be in attendance. With that glint in his eye, he told the whole congregation that she had gotten into his liquor cabinet, and gotten a bit tipsy and fallen down. Immediately a roar of shocked laughter rocked the room.

Most of the congregation knew Arline well and knew she rarely drank. I'm not sure if the congregation was more shocked that she had gotten tipsy, or that Pastor Ed actually had a liquor cabinet. Not in attendance that day, Arline did not hear that story until years later. Pastor Ed's lifelong hobby was boxing, but finally hearing that story, she may have decked him.

A good friend is priceless. In her later years, Arline had some health problems and was not allowed to drive. Occasionally, she would call on Pat to drive her to a medical appointment. Pat was not sure why, but during those trips, Arline placed hourly cell phone calls to Ed. He always commented that as long as she was with Pat, he knew she would be OK. What confidence—if he had only known at the time, they were both lost!

Pat retired from Hope shortly before her 90th birthday. Still a part of the family, she returned often to fill in as organist when needed. Pat discovered a lovely coincidence when she met the new Pastor, Jennifer Schaefer. While Pat was living at the assisted living facility recovering from an illness, Pastor Jen paid her a visit.

They did not serve the congregation at the same time, but found out that they had been neighbors when both lived in Abington, Pennsylvania. Pastor Jen is closer in age to Pat's sons, who attended the same high school. A warm relationship formed between the women, so Pat asked Pastor Jen to officiate over her modest funeral plans. Part of that plan is for Barbara and I to prerecord a final duet with Pat's accompaniment, singing a favorite hymn, *Amazing Grace*.

CHAPTER 13

Pets

———

"Animal Lovers are a special breed of humans.
Generous of spirit, full of empathy, perhaps
a little prone to sentimentality and with
hearts as big as a cloudless sky."

John Grogan

———

John Grogan's quote describes Pat Prentzel perfectly. Though family, friends, and students have always been important to Pat, her animal family has played a significant role in her life. From a young age, she has been an animal lover and we spent several hours reminiscing with great stories of wonderful pets.

For much of her life, she has had a pet dog. As a very young child, when her family lived in rented home, they were not able to have pets. From the time her father was able to hire an architect to design a home of their own, the Wheelers always had a family dog, and often a cat. She chuckled remembering the time when the family cat, who wasn't very smart, got caught in a tree and her dignified father had to perform the undignified act of climbing the tree to rescue it.

Her favorite childhood dog was Wags, whose mischief shortened his life with the Wheelers. After she married and had a home of her own, Pat had a series of dogs. If anyone needed to find a home for a dog, Pat willingly took it off of their hands. She had beagles, collies, dachshunds, and poodles.

One of her more memorable dogs was a whippet named Louie. Despite his size and speed Louie was very much of a lap dog. Louie was sweet, but as his breed indicated, he loved to run. More than once, Pat had to bail him out of doggie jail after he was picked up when he ran off. The local dog catcher remarked that he had never seen a dog run so fast.

When Lady joined the family, they became fast friends. Even though Lady, a beautiful and intelligent sheltie, was not prone to running off, she could be led astray. While they all lived in the farmhouse at the edge of town, Louie tempted Lady to take off on an adventure of their own.

When Pat discovered the dogs were missing, she called everyone she knew, including her friend, Bill, who had helped her select Lady, and then she called the police. They drove around desperately searching for the mischievous dogs. Eventually the dogs were returned home, Lady, a bit sheepish, and Louie, sporting that sweet canine face that melted everyone's heart.

It was about this time that Pat realized she didn't need two large dogs and a cat, and Louie drew the short straw. He was a beautiful dog, so a friend of Pat's volunteered to take him. He didn't stay long. One day when her friend was at work, the smoke alarm went off. Having very sensitive ears as dogs do, Louie went berserk and escaped from the house. After that incident, Pat's friend felt she could not keep him and gave him back to Pat, where he lived until he fell ill and had to be put to sleep.

Her grandson, Nick, sheepishly remembers in a fit of boyish enthusiasm, jumping off some steps and landing on her miniature poodle, breaking the dog's leg. It proved to be a costly stunt, but Pat felt it was worth paying for the surgery to save the dog's leg. Fortunately for Nick, both he and the dog survived.

Her husband, Dave, also enjoyed the dogs, so the family always had a pet, both cats and dogs. During Steve's childhood, they had a beloved cat named Pudgy for a long time, until she became sick with cancer. She had used up all her nine lives and eventually, the cat had to be put to sleep. Even though he was a grown man, Steve was heartbroken, and never fully forgave his mother for the cat's demise.

Her second to the last pet cat liked to be an outside cat, but after having kittens, lost favor with the family when she became infected with fleas. The cat then shared them with Pat's husband and son, Tom. When she finally got rid of the fleas and the cat, Pat figured her cat ownership days were over, but she was wrong.

The best and final cat in her menagerie was a beautiful Russian Blue named Cleopatra. Pat was living in her elegant townhouse in Abington, when she acquired Cleopatra. Having recently and, she thought, finally cleared her home of cats, she also rid herself of all of the paraphernalia associated with cat ownership.

However, one evening two young women came to her door carrying a beautiful large gray cat. They lived nearby in the same housing complex and had determined that Pat's distinctive home was the appropriate new residence for their cat. At first, Pat hesitated, because she had no food, toys, or litter box, but the girls persisted and promised to supply her with the necessary equipment, which they did.

Pat immediately fell under Cleopatra's spell and they were constant companions for many years to follow. Cleopatra had the run of the townhouse. Although the girls had supplied her with plenty of cat toys, she enjoyed leaping up on the dining room table and batting her paws at a crystal chandelier that adorned Pat's dinner table. Pat was able to discourage that behavior, so both the cat and chandelier survived.

Pat's dog, Lady, also fell under Cleopatra's spell. They became fast friends and often cuddled up together to sleep. When Pat left Pennsylvania behind for better weather, both of them accompanied her on the move to Florida.

From the beginning, Cleopatra seemed to take on human qualities. Pat believed that Cleopatra may have been human in a former existence, as she hated the trip, continually getting carsick. Pat finally had to give her pills to make the long drive tolerable. Another of Cleopatra's human characteristics was that she seemed to be a music critic.

She was a constant presence at Pat's sessions with vocal students. As the students arrived for the lesson, Cleo would hop up on the piano bench, and sit beside Pat while she played the piano accompanying the students as they performed their vocal warmups. The cat focused on the student and stared directly at him or her throughout the lesson.

On the other hand, when a piano student entered the house, Cleo would jump down from the bench and scamper off to another room. It wasn't surprising to those who knew her, that she knew the difference as soon as the student walked in the door.

She also seemed to have a sense about people and was known to be relentless, if she wanted to win someone over. At one social event, Pat's friend, who clearly disliked cats, kept his distance. However, Cleo wouldn't accept that. She carefully walked across the back of the sofa, passing three other occupants, until she reached her reluctant prey. There she stopped, only then to demand his attention.

On the other hand, Lady was a smart and affectionate pet and Pat's devoted companion for nearly fifteen years. After the move to Florida, they would take daily evening walks, but Cleopatra never consented to be left behind, so she routinely accompanied them on these walks.

In her old age, Lady lost her hearing. Pat attempted to help by acquiring a canine hearing aid, but Lady never really liked it. Ever protective of her mistress, she followed Pat closely at all times, never losing track of her.

One day while taking a walk, Lady lost consciousness and collapsed in the street. A motorist stopped and offered help, but when Pat asked him if he would put the dog in the car and drive them home, he was hesitant.

Fortunately for Pat, Lady woke up from the faint, and taking care of her mistress one last time, she slowly got to her feet and walked the few short blocks back home on her own. Arriving home, she settled to sleep in her usual spot. Sadly, in the morning, Pat found that Lady had died peacefully in her sleep.

Cleo lived on for several more years, but she became ill and was so sick, she repeatedly threw up. Pat took Cleo to her vet, where she learned the cat had a fatal illness only that was only treatable by taking her to a specialist in another state. Since Cleo was getting on in years, Pat reluctantly realized that, there was little hope, so this wasn't an option. She lovingly allowed the vet to end Cleopatra's suffering.

To this very day, Pat misses both of her friends and often feels their presence. Her final words before she falls asleep each evening are, "Good night, Lady. Good night, Cleo." She has never replaced either one.

CHAPTER 14

Finale But Not Finis

*"We can't always choose the music life plays for us,
but we can choose how we dance to it."*

Unknown

Writing a biographical story is for the writer, full of surprises. I met Patricia Prentzel as she was nearing 80 years old, whereas I was in my mid-50s and at a turning point in my life. Recently retired and relocated to Florida after a lifelong residence in Wisconsin, I was looking for interesting activities to occupy my time, and meet new people.

Pat, the new organist and choir director for the church I attended reached out to me immediately. I was an experienced singer and wanted to become involved in something musical, so I joined the church choir. As she did to all promising singers she met, she extended an invitation to me to join the North Port Chorale, the community chorus that she also directed.

I recognized her as a talented musician and competent director, but had no idea where this new road would take me. The surprises along the way led me to understand that my new journey was only a tiny bud on a branch of Pat's tree of life.

This story is not about me, but in a way, it could be a chapter in *my* autobiography. Writer, speaker, choreographer and vocal soloist were never in my resume until I met Pat. In what I thought would be my retirement, Pat managed to bring out the best in me in a never-ending series of musical and intellectual challenges.

Because she unintentionally changed my life in a way I could not have predicted, I initially asked if I could interview her for a writing project. She enthusiastically accepted my request. My initial goal was to provide us with new topics of conversation when I visited her in the assisted care home where she was temporarily confined.

Following a series of physical health problems, she needed some extra assistance while she healed and recovered. During her stay, she remained as always, mentally sharp with a great sense of humor. After just a few months in assisted living, her immediate goal and personal challenge was to return to her own home.

I, on the other hand, was twenty-four years younger and still leading a busy life, traveling, enjoying my family, and staying involved in local activities. However, I was serious about maintaining contact with her, hoping that I could give back some of the enrichment that she brought to my life.

When I came back to her with tales of my adventures, Pat was always a great listener. Confined to the care facility, she had few new stories to tell me, too. I never want to do all the talking, and I suspected she had a myriad of old stories that I hadn't heard. We met weekly and with each visit, I was amazed and surprised at her revelations.

We laughed more than we cried. Separated by geography and a generation, we found many parallels in our lives. We were both daughters with strong father figures, college educated, wives, mothers, entrepreneurs, teachers, travelers, and sports women. However, it was the music, which brought us together and then cemented our friendship.

At age 97, due to a weakness in her left arm, Pat had some difficulty playing the piano. She still encouraged me to bring some sheet music to our meetings and continued to work on improving my voice. She wanted me to avoid bad habits I may have formed in an absence of her regular instruction.

While Pat was in assisted living, I tried to think of something to brighten her dreary days when I visited. Since she was not particularly enjoying the meals in the facility, I figured an occasional treat of home-baked cookies would be welcome. Even when she returned home, it became a weekly ritual for us. "Cookie Day" often reflected what was happening in my life as well. I tried to alternate recipes, but soon discovered which ones were her favorites. My husband really loved Cookie Day as well, since he was the recipient of any leftovers.

I knew her as a choir and chorale director, voice teacher, and finally as a close friend. At age 98, her mind was still sharp and she still takes very little medication. However, due to the Covid Pandemic restrictions, a huge disappointment to both of us was that I had to discontinue my weekly voice lessons.

We had become more than just teacher and student. At the end of each lesson, we were able to relax in her living room and spend some time chatting about our daily lives. We were often joined by Barbara Johnson, who had a session scheduled after mine. Pat patiently listened to both our stories about our busy lives, and often related stories of her past. As a result of these chats, we all knew there were more stories to tell.

Barbara has a beautiful soprano voice and a great deal more performance experience than I did. We are nearly the same age and became singing buddies. Pat clarified that she taught me, but she really just coached Barbara. I was honored that Barbara consented to sing duets with me. We both worked diligently at blending our voices. I never cared to be a soloist, so the duets were always my favorite part of the lessons.

After several years of weekly sessions, Pat challenged Barbara and me to put together a recital. Under Pat's guidance, we both worked for several months choosing and preparing our best songs. In my life, I have never worked harder at many endeavors. At age 68, this was my first and only solo recital.

It was a mental and physical challenge for both Barbara and me. I would come home exhausted, but encouraged after our weekly practice sessions. One sunny March afternoon, in the sanctuary of Hope Lutheran Church, before an audience of close friends, Barbara and I each performed about ten songs each and intermingled four duets into the program. To complement our soprano and mezzo voices, we were joined by a dear friend and tenor, the late Dick Gates, who also entertained the audience with a few of his favorite numbers.

At that time, I was so used to Pat accompanying me on the piano that I clearly didn't realize or appreciate what a privilege it was to have such a capable and talented accompanist. Moreover, I didn't recognize what a physical effort it was for her. My dear friend; Margie, who was in her mid-80s, and also played the piano, attended the recital. Following the performance, she commented that it was amazing that for ninety minutes, at age 92, Pat sat on a backless piano bench and without a break, flawlessly accompanied all of our numbers, never missing a note.

Of all the chapters of her life Pat tells me she finds teaching the most rewarding, but performing was the most exciting. It's my hope she found a bit of both that day.

Throughout my life I have had the good fortune to receive instruction from a few great teachers. I count Pat among those. She is intelligent, analytical, critical, and relentless. She softens her critiques with a deep sense of empathy and a wonderful sense of humor. It has been my pleasure and I hope hers to be her student and friend.

CHAPTER 15

We All Need a Little Help Sometimes

"You may not control all the events that happen to you, but you can decide not to be reduced by them."

Maya Angelou

Throughout her long life, Pat became accustomed to making most of her major life's decisions on her own. She has also overcome many obstacles, but the one that she cannot overcome is her own mortality.

Although throughout her life, she has been blessed with good health and at age 90, she lived independently in her Florida home and continued to teach piano and voice lessons to a few adult students.

Those lessons became part of her social life, and often after the session, she and Barbara or I loved to relax and tell stories following the lessons. Pat is a great listener, and we knew well that anything told her in confidence would not go any further.

Retired from directing, she finally had more leisure time to spend with friends and family. She is an avid bridge player and played regularly until the Covid pandemic ended those gatherings. It was an important part of her weekly schedule, and she enjoyed giving her opponents in their 70s and 80s a run for their money.

As she entered her mid-nineties, a series of physical problems slowed her down and temporarily robbed her of her independence. She attributes her healthy memory to many years of memorizing complex musical compositions.

After a short hospital stay, the necessity of temporarily entering assisted living was an unwelcome consequence. Previously, she had been able to heal and then return home in a few days or weeks. After a fall however, she needed some additional assistance, so she entered The Springs, an assisted living facility in North Port, Florida.

However, Pat soon grew restless. Even though she could be surrounded by a few pieces of her own furniture and some personal items, it wasn't the same as living in her own home with the privacy and comfort it afforded.

She wasn't fond of the food, but mealtimes did provide a regular social contact in the dining room with other residents. About this time, Covid-19 lockdowns ended visitations from outside friends and family, which at least would have made the situation somewhat more bearable.

Conversations with other residents became her only face-to-face social contact. However, depending on her companion's level of dementia, they could be tedious and repetitive.

Also, the staff continually turned over, so she had no chance of forming any familiarity with the people who were allowed to enter her room. Another issue was that during this time, masks were required for all staff, so recognizing people was nearly impossible.

Almost immediately, she questioned her physician as to how long she needed to remain in assisted living. After a few months in which her body healed, her physician could no longer justify any medical reason for her to remain confined at The Springs.

Hearing this positive news, her natural determination reawakened and she began planning to return home. However, she was realistic and realized that she needed help overcoming the complexities of moving her furniture and possessions home.

Her son, Tom, who had been managing her affairs, did not expect this turn of events, so he was not at all supportive in these efforts. She also was aware that, although she did not need or want a full-time companion, she would need some assistance at home with a few of the basic activities of daily life. Unsteady on her feet at times, she knew shopping, housekeeping, and personal care would be challenging.

Unfortunately, at this difficult time in her life, her son let her down. He had problems of his own, so he was not willing to help his mother in her transition from assisted living back to her own home.

Never wanting to burden her friends, Pat experienced extreme frustration, until Eric, a close friend of Tom's, offered his help in making arrangements. As a boy, Eric had been a regular visitor to the Prentzel house.

Being the best of friends, the boys spent most of their after-school afternoons together. Due to the ongoing piano and vocal lessons that often occupied late afternoons in the Prentzel house, the boys usually were in one door and out the other after school, mostly retreating to Eric's house.

Eric came from a lively family of four boys, but his mother was at home to keep tabs on the boys. As adults, Eric and Tom went their separate ways, but kept in touch over the years. Eric finished college and obtained a masters' degree in business. Pat describes him as good looking and personable, and he had been successful in business throughout his career. He often stopped in to see her when he visited his friends and family in Florida.

When Eric heard of Pat's confinement, he kindly called and checked in on her. His calls were welcome and Pat spoke fondly of him and referred to him as her third son.

When she told him that she was anxious to leave the assisted living facility, he asked if he could be of any help. Pat willingly accepted his offer, so Eric took charge and hired movers to take her belongings back home.

Then, he arranged for a homecare service two days a week, so Pat could feel secure and comfortable when she returned. Grateful for his help, Pat moved home and began the next phase of her life, living with grace and dignity in independence once more.

Hiring homecare help has its challenges as well. Eric lives out of state, so even though he checked in regularly, he couldn't always solve day-to-day problems. Finding and keeping a reliable caregiver became an ongoing challenge. The company Eric employed to send a caregiver for a few days a week worked out only temporarily.

Her first assistant, Lesley, was a warm and compassionate woman in her early 60s, so Pat thought she had hit the jackpot having Lesley in her life. She was comfortable with limited visits two days a week. Lesley was capable and experienced, so she efficiently and easily accomplished what Pat needed in that amount of time. Unfortunately for Pat, the agency that employed Lesley had other plans for her. Those other activities soon took precedence with her employer and they pulled her from Pat's service. Neither Lesley nor Pat was happy about it, so Pat had to find an alternative solution to her situation.

On her own again, Pat had to seek out and hire another company to provide the service she needed. South Florida has a significant elderly population, so there is no shortage of available agencies. Pat personally interviewed several companies and finally found one that she hoped would send a capable helper.

It's not just a cliché that it's hard to find good help. For some caregivers, getting dishes into the dishwasher and laundry out of the dryer was above and beyond the call of duty. Reading a simple shopping list was a task that stymied others. After returning from a shopping trip, one caregiver put all the frozen food in the refrigerator. Fortunately, Pat noticed the error and avoided a defrosting disaster.

Her most amusing complication happened one day when the scheduled assistant did not show up at the appointed time. Pat called and pleaded with the agency to send a person who would at least help her take a shower. When Pat answered her door later in the day, a large muscular young man stood on her doorstep.

When he identified himself as her latest assistant, Pat was stymied as to what she should do. Not wanting to doubt his qualifications or insult him, but knowing this was a bad idea, Pat hesitantly asked him if he was the one sent to help her take a shower. Awkwardly, he stammered that possibly the agency had gotten the directions mixed up once more. They both agreed that his employer needed to send a more appropriate caregiver.

Eric got the ball rolling for Pat's return home, but when she arrived home, her grandson, Nick, who lived nearby, had to assume the task of handling some of her affairs. She lovingly states how proud she is of him! In the era of the Covid-19 pandemic, many friends were reluctant to visit a 96-year-old woman in person.

Pat has always felt close to Nick, and the feeling is mutual. They often reminisce with stories of his childhood. Nick accepted the responsibility of taking the time to visit and helped her to make short trips from the house. He was willing to spend part of his only day off from work. A few times, he even drove her to appointments and took her on brief shopping excursions.

Like Pat, Nick grew up near his grandmother and formed that special bond. His parents had divorced when he was a young boy, so he was mostly raised by his mother. Pat maintained a good relationship with Nick's mother, Jan, who was Tom's ex-wife.

Jan lived near them and was fortunate to be able to spend time with Nick. She regularly attended his little league baseball and football games. She was also on the spot early in his teenage years to help out when the apartment building where he lived with his mother was destroyed by fire.

Nick stayed with Pat until life returned to normal. All of Nick's possessions were destroyed in the fire, so taking pity on him, his schoolmates took up a collection of used clothing to help out. Nick did not want their pity or their charity, so he refused to wear his friends' hand-me-down clothes. Pat saved his pride and bought him several outfits until his situation returned to normal. He had lost all of his clothing and possessions, including a set of golf clubs. However, Nick was saddened the most by the loss of his beloved pet parakeet.

From the time he was a teenager, Nick has been interested in baking. He worked in a bakery and began to learn the trade while still in high school. Pat remembers being treated to many wonderful creations. That passion eventually led to the responsible position of bakery manager for a large supermarket chain in Florida.

Despite the demands of job and family, he remains devoted to his Nana, Pat. His reliability provided comfort and security and allowed Pat to maintain her independence once more.

Pat is also is a great comfort to Nick. Following the untimely death of his mother, Pat was an empathetic sounding board as he struggled to cope with his grief. His visits were a comfort to them both.

The nature of Nick's job required him to often work odd hours and leave town to offer his assistance when a new store was opening. The obligations of raising a large family consumed most of his free hours as well, so Nick found it increasingly difficult to spend time visiting Pat.

After a series of unsatisfactory attempts at finding capable help, Pat's life was improved greatly by the return of her first caregiver, Lesley. She is devoted to Pat's continued comfort and security in her own home. Pat also appreciates Lesley's astute attention to her needs and capable organization of her household.

At 96, Pat's life should have settled into a relaxed routine, living in her own home with Lesley's help. She looks forward to visits from friends and welcomes cards and calls. With Lesley's help, she is able to leave home for routine medical visits and enjoys regular trips to the beauty shop. However, in September of 2022, Hurricane Ian arrived on the scene and forever changed the lives of most residents of several counties in southwest Florida.

CHAPTER 16

The Hurricane of the Century

---

*"Hurricane season brings a humbling reminder
that, despite our technologies, most of
nature remains unpredictable."*

Diane Ackerman

Hurricane Ian was named by the local press, "The Hurricane of the Century." I had saved some newspapers from the days following Hurricane *Charley* in August of 2004, which at that time was also described in the same terms. Hurricane Ian followed the same path as Hurricane Charley, coming onshore on the Gulf Coast of Florida at Cayo Costa State Park. This is a barrier island located between the famous resort towns of Sanibel and Boca Grande, so it caused devastating destruction to those islands. The difference, hurricane experts declared, was that Ian was so large that Charley could have fit within its eye.

"I've lived in Florida since 1996, so I've lived through a lot of hurricanes." Pat calmly remarked when I visited her following Hurricane Ian in late September of 2022. "I think that we were so stunned by all the destruction around us that we just watched it happen. There was really nothing we could do."

The storm had been predicted to be massive and probably rated as a category 3 or 4 hurricane as it was heading up the gulf coast of Florida. The various weather forecast models showed it could possibly make landfall near Tampa, Florida, or farther north. Like most folks who have spent a few decades in Florida, Pat figured there was no reason to panic until the final path was headed towards her doorstep.

Regardless of the expected outcome, preparation for a hurricane event is crucial. With modern meteorological models, a person has several days to prepare. Lesley, Pat's companion, made careful plans to weather the storm and the possible power outages that often follow. The tension built as they listened to the ominous predictions on the television news. Armed with batteries, bottled water, charged cell phones, a cooler full of ice, and easily prepared nonperishable food supplies, they hunkered down together in Pat's home to wait for the storm to arrive.

The first unpleasant surprise as the hurricane approached was that the power went off about 5:00 a.m. the morning of September 28, 2022. Pat awoke earlier than usual, before the sun came up, and found herself in the dark. When the storm had been first predicted to possibly hit close by, Lesley had kindly promised that she would stay with Pat during the duration to be certain that her basic needs were met, and that neither one would have to be alone during the storm.

As predicted, Hurricane Ian slowly lumbered up Florida's gulf coast. Lesley arrived at Pat's home the night before the storm was predicted to make landfall, and decided to stay. Little did they both know at the time that they would be constant companions for days. They were trapped in Pat's house by flood waters that rose in the streets of North Port, and did not recede until a nearly a week later. However, Pat's house was properly elevated, so no flood waters entered the house.

By the time the sun should have risen that day, the rain was falling in a steady downpour. In the deepening gloom with increasingly gusty winds, smaller trees and bushes were already leaning over, straining against the now constant winds. Without any electrical power, Lesley and Pat sat in the dark as they watched loose objects begin to blow around the neighborhood.

About noon, the winds picked up significantly and Pat could hear and observe the outside world begin to collapse around her. By midafternoon, the heavy downpour of rain, now blowing sideways, made visibility outside nearly impossible. The howling wind and the driving rain of this relentless storm lasted well into the evening. Pat and Lesley patiently waited for the calm of the eye of the storm, which never arrived. Instead, the eye wall, with the strongest winds, lingered over the area for several hours. The slow-moving hurricane seemed like it would never move on.

Throughout the neighborhood, large palms and other trees, which in the past have withstood hurricane force winds, were snapped off or torn out by the roots, many dropping on rooftops. In the dark, they could hear branches and pieces of debris hitting the house. Fortunately, Pat's roof was basically sound and did not fail. However, she did lose some shingles and later discovered some minor leaks.

As darkness approached that fateful day, the wind still howled. Everyone who had not evacuated grew very weary of the storm. They began to feel that their world might never be the same. It wasn't until late in the evening that the wind relented and the rain finally let up.

When the winds finally died down, massive damage and flooding quickly became evident. Lesley peered out the window in Pat's bedroom where they had spent most of the storm, and saw intrepid neighbors floating up and down the street in small boats. The local police rode by in airboats to check out the neighborhood. Pat and Lesley could only fall into a fitful sleep, completely unaware of what the next day would bring.

The first light of the following morning revealed a surprisingly pleasant sunny, cool, and breezy September day. It also revealed a wave of destruction no one had anticipated. In the initial days after the storm, electrical power was off, so there was no air conditioning and running water had dropped to a trickle. When the water pressure returned to normal, no one was really sure if the water was safe to drink. The whole city was on a boil water notice.

Without a working electric range or microwave, cooking was a difficult task. Somewhat prepared for this situation, Lesley improvised and brewed Pat's tea with bottled water on a tiny sterno burner. Any foods that needed to be cooked had to be prepared in the same manner. No word was given as to the restoration of power, so the refrigerator became useless. Most of their fresh food had to be discarded.

During and immediately following the storm, communication with the outside world was next to impossible. Normally, Pat's main source of news and entertainment was cable television and the local newspaper. Without power or cable service, the television was useless and, with the roads flooded, no newspapers could be delivered.

Cellular service, everyone's alternate source of news and communication with the rest of the world, was also sporadic for the first few days following the hurricane. Those calls either did not connect or were cut off after a brief connection. Cell phone texting was the only reliable means of communication. Pat and Lesley spent several days alone without power, and in very limited communication with friends and family.

A few days later, Pat's niece, Stephanie, was able to make contact with her aunt. Hearing the news, and realizing her desperate situation, she invited Pat to come and stay at her home in Seminole, Florida. Seminole was outside the area of widespread destruction, so Stephanie still had electrical power and did not suffer any damaging effects from the storm.

It took Stephanie and her husband, Gene, two attempts to drive to Pat's house. The first attempt was thwarted when, following the storm, rising water from the Myakka River flooded the interstate highway just to the north of North Port. When the flood waters receded, they finally were able to navigate the roads on Saturday following Wednesday's storm.

Gene was also very helpful and temporarily covered Pat's roof with a tarp until the proper repairs could be made. He also cleared away much of the debris and trimmed damaged bushes, so that her property took on a semblance of order.

It was a surprise to Stephanie and Gene that Lesley would also be going home with them. Lesley's apartment had also been heavily damaged by wind and water, so her landlord declared she should not return immediately. Graciously, Stephanie's family welcomed them both for a short visit.

In recent months, this area of southwest Florida had been experiencing a building boom, so most of the legitimate contractors who could provide roofing, electrical service, drywall, and plumbing had been very busy with new construction. However, with thousands of homes damaged, finding qualified people to come in and perform small jobs or make minor and major repairs was a challenge.

The local authorities raised the awareness for residents, cautioning them to be careful of unscrupulous or unlicensed contractors who were invading the state and taking advantage of unsuspecting desperate people with homes that were so badly damaged that many had been deemed unsafe or unlivable.

Pat's home had withstood the storm, so when the power and water were restored a week later, her daily activities of life generally could return to normal. After spending a week in Seminole, she and Lesley were able and grateful to return home.

I was able to visit them again, allowing Lesley to leave to take care of her other responsibilities. However, Lesley's home was still so badly damaged that she could not return there to live. Pat generously invited her to stay until she could safely return to her own place.

Having suffered some damage to her roof that had been replaced after Hurricane Charley in 2004, Pat now had to contact her insurance company to file a claim. The insurance company's initial response was to send an adjuster to inspect the damage, when the first hurdle presented itself.

The adjuster showed up, but did not like Gene's tarping technique and would not make the necessary report until it was remedied. Except for that minor inconvenience, Pat found that her insurance company acted responsibly, contacted a roofing company directly, and was willing to pay for a complete roof replacement.

In the end, Pat considered herself lucky. With thousands of Florida residents in the same situation, repairs were delayed indefinitely for many homeowners and businesses, some taking months or even years.

Fortunately, southwest Florida experienced a normally dry fall, so Gene's tarping held up. Pat's home was spared from any further internal damage from the storm until her roof was finally replaced several months later.

The final meteorological analysis showed Hurricane Ian to be a solid category 4 and possibly even a 5 in some areas. Unlike many of her less fortunate friends and neighbors, Pat's life and home were returned to normal just before the arrival of the next hurricane season, which officially begins June 1st.

A Word From the Author

Early on in our journey together in writing this book, Pat told me that in a lifetime of music, she found that teaching was rewarding, but performing was exciting. As a young person, she spent her time, first listening to others, and then exploring and developing her own talent. Her midlife job was to raise her family and impart to her students, both children and adults, the knowledge and experience gained in those years.

As she entered what should have been retirement, she added wisdom and experience to that knowledge and continued to inspire others to excellence. She has been an inspiration to those who were looking to get the most from retirement and taught us to never stop learning and improving. Many friends and former students still come to her for advice on many topics, not always related to music.

During all the phases of her life, she may have changed her methods, but her philosophy remained and became stronger with age and wisdom. "Focus your talents for Good," she reminded me. She has seen talented people fall into the ego trip of fame and money and forget that their gifts were God-given.

Throughout her life, her mission as teacher and director was to be an inspiration to people who have the desire, but possibly not the confidence to perform. Being shy as a child herself, she never dreamed of being a performer.

Her parents were an inspiration to her in that respect. Her mother had a wonderful operatic voice and a charming personality to match. She showed her daughter that life could be full of music. She performed and gave joy to others, while raising strong and capable children.

Pat observed and learned from her mother and lost her shyness along the way. Her father was intelligent and driven professionally, but took the time to instill in his daughter the spirit to strive for excellence in any endeavor she pursued.

During her college career, Dr. Lloyd Mitchell was, in Pat's words, "a wonderful teacher." He was proud of his protégé and showed it by inviting her back to join him professionally as an instructor at West Chester College. The alumni association of West Chester University also recognized Pat Prentzel's career and influence by honoring her in 2022 as one of their Distinguished Alumni of the year.

Following her sheltered college experience, Katherine Frost grabbed a hold of Pat's career as a concert pianist by introducing her to the larger world of professional stage performance and expanded her audience by hundreds of admirers.

It must have been a disappointment to leave that world and adulation of the large audience, but Pat gave it up to devote herself to her husband and family. However, she didn't give up performing—the audiences just became smaller, but often were just as appreciative.

When she entered the world of classroom teaching, she passed on knowledge to willing and unwilling participants. A few years ago, she discovered a book written by a former student, who became a successful band director. It pleased her to know she could have been his inspiration to teach well. When I asked about her philosophy of teaching, she said, "You need to have a thorough knowledge of your subject and the personality to impart it to others."

She sees directing as teaching in a different format. When directing groups of adults, such as her church choirs and the chorale, she said, "I could tell who was into this and who wasn't. Some just loved to sing, and it didn't matter what they were singing."

When working with adults, she learned that affability is important. "In addition to that friendly good-natured manner, you do have to be a bit aloof. As a director, you are not singing with the group—you are inspiring others to recognize that the music is what is important." In all the years I knew Pat as director, she never attempted to upstage her ensemble.

As in anyone's life, there have been a few people who have disappointed her. It was Pat's choice to leave out the names of people who wronged her and ignore some of the unpleasant details of her past, which have led to anger and disappointment. To this day, she follows her own advice to set negativity aside and focus on the positive. Her philosophy is, "Use negativity to build your own character."

In listening to and relating her story, I learned that Pat is an astute listener. Her memory is largely intact and she will often ask me about details of conversations in the recent past. She always asks about my family, whom she has never met.

Her many calls and visitors reflect that a visit by phone or in person is always time well spent for both participants. In telling me her story, she has learned as much about my life as I have of hers.

It is been my joy and privilege to share her story.

Printed in the USA
CPSIA information can be obtained
at www.ICGtesting.com
LVHW071425160824
788363LV00015B/446

9 781614 939641